THE DOLPHIN

General Editor: Tim Caudery

24

SCREEN SHAKESPEARE

Edited by Michael Skovmand

AARHUS UNIVERSITY PRESS

Word-processed at the Department of English, Aarhus University
Printed in the UK by Cambridge University Press
ISBN 87 7288 375 8
ISSN 0106 4487

The Dolphin no. 24

Published with financial support from the Danish Research Council
for the Humanities

Editorial address:
The Dolphin
Department of English, Aarhus University
DK-8000 Aarhus C, Denmark

Distribution:
Aarhus University Press
Building 170, Aarhus University
DK-8000 Aarhus C, Denmark
Fax: + 45 86 19 84 33

Cover illustration: Detail of poster for Kenneth Branagh's *Henry V.*

Contents

Acknowledgements

I would like to thank the following individuals and institutions for their kind assistance, and for permission to use their materials: Pathe-Nordisk, Copenhagen, for permission to use stills from *Hamlet*; Camera Film, Copenhagen, for permission to use stills from *Ran*; the University Research Library, University of California, Los Angeles, for permission to use the Welles' *Macbeth* poster; Peter Greenaway for permission to use prints from his *Prospero's Books* (Chatto & Windus 1991); a special thanks to Loke Havn, Warner Metronome, Copenhagen, for his kind assistance in general, for permission to use the stills from *Henry V*, including the poster still for the cover of this book, and especially for organising an early viewing of Branagh's *Much Ado About Nothing*; finally a special thanks to Tim Caudery for his much appreciated assistance in proofreading, and in general; and to Signe Frits for invaluable technical assistance.

Michael Skovmand

Introduction, with a Discussion on Branagh and *Much Ado*

Michael Skovmand

'Does the world really need another book on nineteenth-century fiction?' said Basil.
'I don't know, but it's going to get one,' said Robyn.

The above exchange, from David Lodge's novel *Nice Work,* came to mind when a colleague of mine made a similar query as to the relevance of yet another collection of essays on Shakespearean films. But *Screen Shakespeare*, however modest its intentions, does see itself as more than a simple addition to the existing body of literature on Shakespeare on film. It is published with a combination of two intentions: one, to provide substantial analyses of recent Shakespearean films (Kurosawa's *Ran*, Branagh's *Henry V*, Stoppard's *Rosencrantz and Guildenstern are Dead*, Zeffirelli's *Hamlet*, and Greenaway's *Prospero's Books*); and two, to provide a number of 'alternative' approaches to established classics (*A Midsummer Night's Dream* – from Reinhardt to Allen; the production process of Welles' *Macbeth*; a revisionist view of Peter Brook's *King Lear*; and a 'reception study' of Polanski's *Macbeth*).

Unlike some recent work,[1] these essays, however diverse in their approaches, are neither apologetic nor defensive in their attitudes towards working with Shakespeare and film. Nor are they overly concerned with being inside or outside a particular canon. If there is a consensus behind this collection of essays, it is to do with seeing the field of Shakespearean film as a simply another fascinating area of creative and critical activity within Shakespeare studies, to the exclusion of neither live theatre nor academic work with the plays in their written forms. Shakespearean film studies are based on what Peter Donaldson calls 'performance retextualized'.[2] We are no longer caught between the virtuality of the playscript and the ephemerality of the performance. Indeed, we are faced with texts with a social life of their own, films which relate in a much more direct way than previous Shakespeare performances to the international marketplace of culture and communications.

The mixed reception of Kenneth Branagh's recent film version of *Much Ado About Nothing* is a good illustration of the peculiar cultural position of Shakespearean films in the marketplace, straddling as they do the great divide between 'high culture' and 'low Hollywood'. In *Time Magazine*, Richard Corliss articulated the dilemma quite succinctly in his review of *Much Ado*: 'This isn't the best Shakespeare on film ... but it may be the best movie Shakespeare' (May 10, 1993).

What, actually, is the difference between Shakespeare on film and 'movie Shakespeare'? Obviously, there is a cultural *distinction*, in the Bourdieu sense of the word, between Shakespeare on film and movie Shakespeare, and, equally obviously, the distinction hinges on the difference between 'film' and 'movie', i.e. the elite notion of art cinema *vs* the popular notion of the movie show. In one word: accessibility. The problematic implication of the *Time Magazine* review is that somehow an inaccessible, i.e. hard to understand, production of Shakespeare is more 'Shakespearean' than an accessible one. Richard Corliss spells it out quite clearly:

> Branagh is a trollop for art. His bold mission is to ensure that everybody – everybody on this planet for whom Shakespeare is unknown or a school punishment – gets it, gets the power and the humor of the poetry, if not its unabridged grandeur. So he encourages Michael Keaton to play Dogberry, the lame-brained lawman, as a veritable triumvirate of Stooges – all spitting and farts and head butts and scrotum grabbing. He wants similarly capitalized emotions from the romantic leads. Go bigger, higher, grander, clearer, he tells them. Speak loud, if you speak love.

Corliss echoes the conventional Platonic notion of a Shakespeare in all his 'unabridged grandeur', unpolluted by interpretation. Curiously, as examples of real Shakespearean films, Corliss quotes Olivier's *Richard III* and Welles' *Chimes at Midnight*, two of the most 'abridged' Shakespearean films ever.

Actually, Branagh does not really disagree with Corliss (if we disregard the snide undertow of the review). He calls his approach the 'reality' approach, a style of acting and directing developed with his Renaissance Theatre Company, and continued in both *Henry V* and *Much Ado*. He has spelt it out most recently in his introduction to the script version of *Much Ado*:

> Ours [i.e. the RTC's] was a style that wished to be in tune with our audience. We were touring around the United Kingdom and Ireland to places and audiences that were also relatively unfamiliar with these plays. Our great joy was to set and tell the story with the utmost clarity and simplicity and let the particular directorial inflection, or interpretation, be seen through the characterizations. In effect, we assumed that no one had seen the play before. We wanted audiences to react to the story as if it were in the here and now and important to them. We did not want them to feel they were in some cultural church.
>
> We made the same attempt in film. The goal was utter reality of characterization. Shakespeare accomplishes this as a matter of course.[3]

Branagh's aim is to combine this clarity of characterization with what he calls 'a bedrock of structural understanding' in order to preserve Shakespeare's 'unique poetry'.

On the face of it, Branagh invites comparison with Franco Zeffirelli, whose *Romeo and Juliet* and *Hamlet* are also largely predicated on this idea of popular accessibility, and whose *Hamlet* in fact gave popular currency to the idea of mixing Shakespearean Brits and American (/Australian) movie stars. (Actually, Branagh was bolder than Zeffirelli, casting-wise, in choosing black Denzel Washingtion for the part as Don Pedro – a move which has triggered no end of academic speculation as to its possible dramatic and political implications).

But the similarity is a surface one. Zeffirelli's approach is largely *melo-dramatic*, with a distinctive sense of *texture* and *mise-en-scène*, but with little sense of an overall interpretive strategy (see the article on Zeffirelli's *Hamlet* in this volume). Branagh, on the other hand, has a clearly worked out strategy of 'adaptation':

> I think that in film terms, it [i.e. adaptation] means giving a strong sense of the interpretive line. In the comedies this is crucial. They must be inflected. They do not lay themselves out with the same strong narrative, historical frame that the history plays do. The very titles themselves invite us to be bold: *Twelfth Night* or *What You Will. As You Like It.*[4]

There is, however, a crucial distinction between Branagh and predecessors such as Orson Welles, Kozintsev, or Kurosawa: However 'bold', Branagh is essentially anti-avantgarde; in fact, far less adventurous than Olivier, with his mix of the cinematic and the deliberately theatrical. But like Laurence Olivier, Branagh is essentially an *adapter*, not an *auteur*.

With the enthusiasm of the recent convert, Branagh rummages about in the cinematic special effects supermarket of Hollywood. But Branagh's productions are not governed by a primarily *audiovisual* concept.

His approach is that of finding the right cinematic *equivalent* of a primarily *theatrical* concept, in which the dynamics of character and verbal delivery are essential ingredients. Now and then, however, this makes the cinematic effects less than organic. A case in point is Branagh's penchant for what Cary Mazer has called the Big Memorable Sequence, or BMS.[5] In *Henry V* there was one BMS – the majestic, slow-motion Non Nobis after the battle of Agincourt. In *Much Ado* there are three. First is the long, semi-slowmotion take of men and women preparing for the homecoming party for the men back from war – a marvellous, if overdone extravaganza of gauzy dresses ripped off, of bouncing breasts and quivering buttocks. BMS no. 2 – less motivated – is on the eve of the final wedding ceremony, with Claudio mourning by Hero's tomb, accompanied by a choir of mourners of Mormon Tabernacle proportions. The third

BMS is the final dance sequence providing the upbeat comedic ending of the film, finishing with a high-angle shot of Tuscany countryside.

Branagh's partiality towards the grandiose *mise en scène* may occasionally lead him astray, but it is carried out with an infectious sense of enthusiasm and commitment of interpretation which make the majority of established Shakespearean films seem stale by comparison. In this context it is curious to observe from 'abroad', i. e. from outside the UK, the ambiguity or downright hostility of much British academic commentary on Branagh. Interestingly, this hostility is not occasioned by his popular, anti-avantgarde approach to Shakespearean film, but by a pervasive unease with his 'politics'. He is seen as a crypto-Thatcherite, an entrepreneur with essentially commercial intentions. As a case in point, his consultations with Prince Charles during the production of *Henry V* were seen by the British intelligentsia as just another instance of Branagh's capacity for entrepreneurial, unprincipled self-promotion. As Graham Holderness puts it in *Shakespeare Recycled*:

> He stands for a reaction against the established national institutions of theatre, such as the Royal Shakespeare Company, and for the development of a privatized theatrical economy, with organizations like his own Renaissance Theatre Company supported by private and corporate sponsorship. Those who also approve of such developments are filled with the passions of admiration when they contemplate Branagh's audacity, energy, ambition, nerve, determination, etc., etc., right through the whole vocabulary of self-help and entrepreneurial capitalism.[6]

In a similar vein of ideological critique, Chris Fitter, in 'A Tale of Two Branaghs: *Henry V*',[7] gives a detailed account of how Branagh's film version of *Henry V* should be seen not as a tough, anti-war, post-Falklands revision of the Olivier version, but, on the contrary, as an ideological *corruption* of the 1984 RSC production:

> ... the 'new' film has in fact tenderly remodelled the critically exploded hagiography of the conservatives, restoring a fellowly, idealized Harry. Its narratological politics are carefully assimilated to those of the mainstream popular culture of the contemporary USA in such a way as to secure Branagh resounding personal success, a commercial Agincourt. Branagh, I suggest, a literary Oliver North, has deliberately shredded vital documentation, provided by the text and the RSC production, and his Henry therefore emerges as a familiar figure: the handsome military hero and godly patriot at the heart of an establishment coverup. (p. 260)

Fitter points out how all the brilliant special features of the film are borrowed from the Noble production: the towering door of the opening scene, Bardolph's execution onstage, the Non Nobis, etc., whereas Branagh's alterations largely consist in idealizing and disambiguating King Henry.

Grudgingly, and in partial contradiction of his previous criticisms, Fitter admits that 'Kenneth Branagh has done us, as lovers of Shakespeare, a quite wonderful cultural service, in giving us a Shakespeare that is genuinely popular, intelligent, and enthralling ...' (p. 274). But, he goes on to say, 'he has done the ordinary people of the English-speaking world ... an irresponsible disservice, in whitewashing traditional autocracy, and the logic of imperialism. What Shakespeare has demystified, Branagh, persuasively, affably, immorally, has resanctified' (pp. 274-75). This, seen from abroad, smacks of parochial political infighting, parallel with the intellectual/political upheaval over the reconstruction of the Globe Theatre and the glorification of Sam Wanamaker. However, in all fairness, it is also a good indication of how Shakespeare/ Bardbiz is still a hotly contested terrain in the disputes over cultural and educational policies in Britain.[8]

Without doubt, Branagh's *Henry V* and *Much Ado About Nothing* have revitalized the domain of Shakespearean film. In secondary and higher education they are of great value as accessible, contemporary interpretations of exemplary clarity and charm. Their potential for moving beyond the art cinema circuit is unquestionable; whether it actually happens depends on factors external to the films, such as the existing possibilities for including such films in the repertoire of mass market cinemas, and the availability of pay film channels on cable television. Branagh's versatility has already led him in several directions, such as the 'art film' *A Month in the Country*, the TV series *Fortunes of War*, the remake *Peter's Friends*, and the Hollywood thriller *Dead Again* but with his already extensive Shakespearean track record in the theatre, there is every reason to believe that he will want to move on to the major comedies and tragedies. If so, he might in time become a welcome alternative to that worthy monument of inert television Shakespeare in the theatre, the BBC Canon. Branagh and the the BBC Canon share the idea of the theatrical concept as a point of departure. Branagh, however, takes us beyond filmed theatre into a species of audiovisual Shakespeare which, at its best, seems to combine some of the most attractive elements of both worlds: the Shakespearean world of words and the cinematic world of motion and spectacle. Indeed, Branagh's approach to filmed Shakespeare is a move away from the often tortured preoccupation with what are seen as radical differences between theatre and film, and a welcome reminder of how much film and theatre actually have in common: a reminder of Shakespeare as the creator of scene and spectacle, dialogue and drama.

Notes

1. See e.g. John Collick, *Shakespeare, Cinema and Society* (Manchester: Manchester University Press 1989), and Graham Holderness, 'Shakespeare Rewound', *Shakespeare Survey* 45, 1993.

The Filmic Tradition of *A Midsummer Night's Dream*: Reinhardt, Bergman, Hall, and Allen

Steven Shelburne

Writing in the mid-1920s, Max Reinhardt diagnosed the 'sterility' of film:

> The art of the film in its present form does not thrive on its own resources and its own strength, although both are available in great abundance. The art is rooted and vegetates on foreign soil. It is a parasite ... of the theatre, of literature, of music, of painting, and so forth. There is no creative film literature; only more or less arbitrary adaptations of dramas, novels, sentimental or detective stories and the like. For this reason, the film can not dispense with the excessive use of the word, although freedom from the word is one of its chief potential characteristics.... The film must create its own new adequate mode of expression. It must open up new springs of composition, performance and music, must live on its own soil, without borrowing everywhere else. It must stand on its own foundation, so that it can dispense entirely with the photographed word.[1]

Reinhardt must still have had many of these deficiencies in mind when, ten years later in 1935, he came to make a film version of *A Midsummer Night's Dream* for Warner Brothers. Few would claim that he overcame the limitations of his new medium, while the ungenerous might say that he only exemplified them with unusual clarity. Still, Reinhardt's production was a cultural phenomenon, and it has always demanded attention. In fact, it is a doubly important film in that it has stimulated both critical and artistic responses. For many critics, Reinhardt initiates the ongoing debate about the artistic and cultural possibilities of Shakespearian film. At the same time, Reinhardt's movie is the first in a series of distinctly filmic versions of *A Midsummer Night's Dream*. It stimulates such directors as Peter Hall and, more recently and surprisingly, Woody Allen, to explore and confront Shakespeare as mediated by Reinhardt.

Reinhardt in Hollywood

Warner Brothers' production of *A Midsummer Night's Dream* was a bid for cultural prestige, and it banked on some substantial reputations.[2] Reinhardt came to the project already famous for his trademark productions of the play and fresh from his successful production at the Hollywood Bowl. When he needed the assistance of a technically proficient filmmaker, Warner assigned William Dieterle to the project. Dieterle had acted under Reinhardt's direction in the Deutsches Theater, and he was now a respected director in his own right.[3] Another renewed association for Reinhardt was Max Ree, who had been the designer for his 1921 production of *A Midsummer Night's Dream* at the Grosses Schauspielhaus in Berlin.[4] Anton Grot, an eventual Academy Award winner who was already with Warner Brothers, served as the Art Director.[5] Bronislava Nijinska and Nini Theilade choreographed the ballets to Mendelssohn's score, arranged by Erich Wolfgang Korngold. Theilade also danced the role of the lead fairy.

To this cadre of European artistic talent Warner Brothers added some of its biggest stars in order to ensure the film's popular appeal. Dick Powell undertook Lysander, Anita Louisa, Titania, and Victor Jory played Oberon. Olivia De Havilland (as Hermia) and Mickey Rooney (as Puck), both hits in Reinhardt's Hollywood Bowl production, came to the film project along with the director. Reinhardt recruited James Cagney to play Bottom and Joe E. Brown for Flute.[6] The film was equally lavish in its budget and production schedule. It cost a million and a half dollars, took seventy days to shoot, and occupied three sound stages.[7] In short, everything about the film was extravagant and high-toned, and Warner Brothers marketed exactly these qualities. The elaborate program distributed to moviegoing audiences immediately calls attention to the film's cultural pretensions. Its cover reads:

WARNER BROS.
PRESENT
Max Reinhardt's
PRODUCTION OF
"A MIDSUMMER
NIGHT'S DREAM"
by
WILLIAM SHAKESPEARE
Music by
FELIX MENDELSSOHN
Arranged by
Erich Wolfgang Korngold

The ballets staged by
Bronislava Nijinska and Nini Theilade
The costumes designed by
Max Ree
Directed by
MAX REINHARDT and WILLIAM DIETERLE

This arrangement emphasizes a tradition of artistry, beginning with Shakespeare and ending with Reinhardt, which includes the contributory arts of music, dance, and design. All of this takes place, of course, under the benign sponsorship of Warner Brothers. Not surprisingly, the program's 'History of the Play' justifies the present production as the culmination of an artistic evolution:

> Because of the opportunities it offers for spectacular presentation, [*A Midsummer Night's Dream*'s] various productions through the ... centuries have been innumerable, and its leading roles have been interpreted by the most famous Shakespearian players of all ages. First rendered by a cast consisting exclusively of male performers and entirely without scenery, its presentations have steadily increased in richness, culminating in Max Reinhardt's brilliant outdoor productions.
> And now on the infinite stage of the screen, Shakespeare and Reinhardt at last find unlimited scope for the complete expression of their imaginative genius.

This great collaboration is enhanced, as further program notes indicate, by the film's 'two remarkable ballets' and its music, which 'is not merely a musical setting, but almost a complete all-Mendelssohn concert'. A companion book, published to coincide with the film's release, contains the full text of Shakespeare's play, a brief 'Forward' by Reinhardt, and is illustrated with 'scenes from the spectacular Warner Brothers production'.[8]

A Midsummer Night's Dream was not a great financial success, nor did it especially need to be. Primarily an investment in prestige, its dividends were to be paid in cultural approbation. And in these terms, the film must be judged successful, if only because it was immediately taken seriously. Many of the issues raised by its early critics remain central to the consideration of Shakespeare on film. Within a year of its release, Allardyce Nicoll used the film to argue the special virtues of the cinematic medium over the stage.[9] Richard Watts, Jr., writing in *The Yale Review*, saw it as an emblem of Hollywood's vacillation 'between Art and Commerce', as did Otis Ferguson, who focused on the contradiction between its alternately reverential and familiar treatment of the Shakespearian script.[10] John Alfred Thomas determined that 'the main effect of this particular translation of Shakespeare into cinema has been to enlarge immeasurably the physical scope of his imagery, lending substance and form to what were merely airy concepts, while throwing into clear relief the utter unsuitability of much of the play to the demands of the screen'.[11] And

Graham Greene, after dismissing as cranks those reviewers who attempted to divine Shakespeare's own reaction to the film, argued that Reinhardt's inexperience with the film medium resulted in 'sequences of great beauty ... [absurdly alternating with] others of almost incredible banality'. Still, Greene liked the film, especially the 'more cinematic fairy sequences ... set to Mendelssohn's music.... this is the way Shakespeare's poetry ought surely to be used if it is not to delay the action. It must be treated as music, not as stage dialogue tied to the image of the speaker like words issuing from the mouth of characters in a cartoon'.[12]

Filmic Responses: Hall and Allen

Besides provoking such critical discussion of Shakespeare on film, itself an important accomplishment, Reinhardt's A Midsummer Night's Dream has in-spired several subsequent filmic treatments of the play. Peter Hall, for ex-ample, in his film version with the Royal Shakespeare Company (1969), tried carefully to avoid Reinhardt's theatrical artifice:

> I've tried in The Dream to get away completely from the expected Shakespearean setting, which is essentially nineteenth century and Pre-Raphaelite. The kind of approach associ-ated with Mendelssohn's incidental music. That's how The Dream has always been pre-sented, culminating in Reinhardt's stage productions, and his film of the 1930s.[13]

Hall insists that his own 'film is not intended as a reproduction of a stage presentation' (p. 126). He is fully aware of the technical opportunities of his new medium, especially of the 'physical closeness' (p. 121) of the camera and its ability to present a selective reality. But despite these protestations, and despite the overriding differences between Hall's film treatment of the play and Reinhardt's, their productions share one crucial similarity: their key ante-cedents are stage productions. Commenting on his fidelity to the language of the text, Hall makes just this point:

> The trouble is that the theatre in the nineteenth century went in for rhetoric, the set-piece recitation. I believe in the other school of acting, that of powerful restraint – what Anna Magnani, for example, was doing here the other week in La Lupa. Or what Duse, one imagines from the accounts of her and her film clips, must have done as distinct from Bernhardt. So when one is filming, the closeness of the camera is no embarrassment. It is, in fact, a support. It insists on thoughtful speech! My company working in The Dream already appreciated this because of the work they had done with me in the theatre. All we had to do was make sure the faces did nothing excessive in expression during the close shots. (p. 122)

Thus the camera perfects a technique learned in the study and developed on the stage. Hall simply can't help thinking of the play in terms of the stage. For all of his innovation, he still belongs to a tradition of directors of Shakespearian film who first learned their craft in the theater and who then brought their understanding to film. This is not to deride Hall's accomplishment; in many ways his *Midsummer Night's Dream* is the most original of film treatments.[14] Rather, it is to point out that the break with the theater tradition is even more problematical than directors sometimes allow. Hall, at his most candid, is blunt: 'To make an absolutely conventional film, with a fully developed film technique, is impossible in the case of Shakespeare, since too much normal film art contradicts the technique of the plays, at least as far as their most important element, the text, is concerned' (p. 125). This is the point that Reinhardt had made forty-five years earlier.

Woody Allen's *A Midsummer Night's Sex Comedy* (Orion, 1982) marks an important departure from the tradition of Reinhardt and Hall even as, indeed because, it recycles their film versions of *A Midsummer Night's Dream* rather than relying on a stage tradition. Allen's antecedents are essentially filmic, and the devices he borrows from his predecessors have been naturalized by them. The theater traditions to which the earlier versions allude (sometimes unwittingly), and which they in some ways summarize, are distanced by earlier filmmakers, and so they have become part of the 'creative ... literature' of the new medium. As a version of *A Midsummer Night's Dream*, Allen's film marks the independence of the Shakespearian story from theater. And with this independence comes a certain license to alter formerly canonical texts, a freedom long felt in the theater but often in practice disallowed to Shakespearian films.[15]

But of course Allen's film is not, in any strict sense, a 'version' of Shakespeare's play. It is not really even an adaptation. It doesn't use Shakespeare's text; it doesn't use his characters; it doesn't follow his plot. Allen seems to take Hall's advice to 'throw away the text altogether ... and develop the fable with all its atmosphere' (p. 125). Still, Allen's clearly allusive title, *A Midsummer Night's Sex Comedy*, apparently insists on a connection; it seems to require the spectral presence of Shakespeare. However, Allen's allusion is best understood not as to the Shakespearian text, but rather to the films that had already become part of a nearly fifty-year-long film tradition, including most obviously Bergman's *Smiles of a Summer Night*. For Allen, these films are the texts that supplant the Shakespearian original.

A Midsummer Night's Sex Comedy sounds at first like a post-Freudian Dream, Shakespeare's play read through Freud's *Interpretation of Dreams*. The film is full of Freudianisms. Early on, Andrew humorously accuses his friend and physician Maxwell of satyriasis: 'you're like one of those characters in Greek mythology who's half goat'. Soon Andrew confesses his marital problems to Maxwell in a fantastic account of sublimation and an inversion of dreams of flying: 'what I do is pour all of my energy into my inventions, you know, because of my problems in bed with her I can now fly'. Maxwell offers modern therapy: 'you know they're doing some amazing things with hypnosis these days in Europe'. Toward the end of the film, Leopold (like Adam) awakens to find his dream of Dulcy come true, a case of wish-fulfillment. And Adrian's confession of her affair with Maxwell therapeutically relieves her guilt and restores her sexual appetite.

Such Freudian concerns, so pervasive in the culture that they need no single source, might still be traced to Allen's preoccupation with Bergman.[16] As many reviewers of *A Midsummer Night's Sex Comedy* noted, Allen's film looks back to Bergman's *Smiles of A Summer Night* (1955) as a precedent. Allen's title seems particularly to acknowledge the genre of boudoir farce that Bergman's *Smiles* exploits and transcends. Allen also adopts the country house setting, the period, and the particular geometry of mismatched couples who promise to find their proper mates. As in *Smiles*, the nap before dinner (when Lawyer Egerman unconsciously admits his love for Desire) becomes a time of revelation (when Leopold plans to meet Dulcy and Maxwell hopes to meet Ariel). In both films these meetings are reprised and eventually sorted out after a dinner party, outdoors, on a moonlit summer night. In both, a rationalist (Egerman/Leopold) is forced to confront a competing part of his own nature; and the young emotive man (Maxwell/Henrik) bungles his suicide and thereby, accidentally, gets the girl.

More compelling than such parallels in plot is how Bergman's film might serve as a precedent in the way it treats Shakespeare. Bergman knew *A Midsummer Night's Dream* from his experience directing it at his Citizen's Theater in Stockholm early in his career.[17] The production was a failure, but Bergman evidently learned from the experience, and he reused the Shakespearian material in *Smiles of a Summer Night*. Stanley Cavell thinks that 'the film's faithfulness to itself justifies the self-confident wittiness of its references to *A Midsummer Night's Dream* (the young lovers communicate through a chink in the wall – the bed moved from one room into another; the girl passes out from spells and the confusion of adults in conflict, and then finds her true love in the young ass she first sees upon awakening; as they flee, her scarf floats from the carriage, with the idea of her virgin's blood on it, dead to her old husband)'.[18] Like Reinhardt and Hall, Bergman begins as a theater director. But when he uses *A Midsummer Night's Dream* in film, it is as part of a new and independent story, not merely an adaptation. Allen uses a similar technique, and he has the advantage of having films, including Bergman's own, as the basis for his allusions.

Allen's use of Bergman combines with references to Hall's production, most obviously the upstate retreat that parallels Hall's English country house setting and Bergman's Ryarp Castle (the country estate of Mrs. Armfeldt). Allen's characters, like Hall's and Bergman's, live in a recognizably natural world, one in which, for instance, they actually get wet and muddy. The most telling allusion to Hall's film, however, is Leopold's recitation of part of Titania's speech about disrupted nature: 'the spring, the summer,/ The childing autumn, angry winter, change/ Their wonted liveries' (II.1.111-13). This is the only direct quotation from Shakespeare's play in Allen's film, and is an especially significant one. Its complete inanity renders it memorable. The very inappropriateness of the line – spoken on a beautiful summer's day when there is no indication of confusion in nature – calls attention to its function as allusion. Hall's film had, in fact, taken Titania's speech as its starting point:

> *The Dream* is quite clearly a play about an English summer in which the seasons have gone wrong. It is winter when it should be summer; everywhere is wet and muddy. This is described by Titania in a central speech [II.1.81-117] This is why I shot much of the film in the rain, during a bad-weather period lasting about six weeks. Titania's speech explaining this has often been cut in the past, yet it is the essence of the situation. (p. 123)

Allen's benign environment marks the distance from Hall's conceptions of the story. The quotation serves as a declaration of difference; debts are acknowledged by allusive contrast.

Woody Allen's allusions to the work of his predecessors indicate that he fully intends to violate the prototypical form of *The Dream*. In his counter-dream there are no weddings; there is not even the usual final symmetry of couples. Instead, a single, unpaired, but entirely self-sufficient woman is left to look out for her own interests. In an important scene, Dulcy returns to the house with a bow and a quiver of arrows, imaged both as randy Diana (a complex of moon imagery) and as an Amazon, the match to Leopold's skeptical Theseus. In moves reminiscent of Bergman, Allen makes Leopold the central character, and identity becomes a central theme as we watch him shed his rationalist defenses. While Allen rejects Bergman's conclusion that a lost love can be regained, he endorses the view that imagination can overcome empirical limitations. In Allen's film, lionizing philosophers turn into pixies.

Allen and Reinhardt

However dependent on the work of Bergman and Hall, Allen's most pervasive debt is to Reinhardt's 1935 production. Allen's use of the Mendelssohn score is the most obvious similarity. Like Reinhardt, Allen gives an opening credit 'Music by Felix Mendelssohn'; but where Reinhardt also gives an arranging credit to Erich Wolfgang Korngold, Allen's audience is left to infer that Allen is himself responsible for making the selections from Mendelssohn. Reinhardt had used the score extensively but conventionally: the Overture for the opening credits, with the introductory chords introducing the moon image; the Scherzo for the awakening of the woods and the dance of the fairies; the Nocturne ('con molto tranquillo') for the 'Flight of the Moonlight' ballet; and the Wedding March for the return of the lovers to Athens and the marriage procession. He also added portions of other Mendelssohn works ('Songs without Words' and the 'Italian' [Op. 90] and 'Scottish' [Op. 56] symphonies).

Though he still gives us nearly an 'all-Mendelssohn concert', Allen reverses the pieces that frame Reinhardt's film. He uses the Wedding March over the opening credits (for there is no wedding in Allen's film) and the Overture (with the introductory chords accompanying the incipient movement of the 'spirit ball') over the closing credits. In between, Allen too uses the Scherzo from the incidental music to *A Midsummer Night's Dream* and selections from the 'Scottish' symphony (second movement, 'vivace non troppo'), as well as parts of the Violin Concerto in E minor (Op. 64, third movement) and the Piano Concerto No. 2 in D minor (Op. 40, second movement). Perhaps most significantly, Allen incorporates non-Mendelssohnian music for the purposes of characterization. Leopold sings two *lieder*, one each by Schubert ('Wohin?' from *Die Schöne Müllerin*) and Schumann ('Ich grolle nicht,' from *Dichterliebe*), and follows these with 'something devotional', Malotte's setting of 'The Lord's Prayer'. The joke here depends on our knowing that both of these *lieder* are parts of romantic song cycles about lost love, the first song about a singing brook animated by water nymphs, the second about a forlorn lover-dreamer. Empathetic nature and the transcendent are entirely alien to Leopold's philosophy. The music denotes a basic contradiction in his character, and perhaps a stage in his changing identity.

The inversion of Reinhardt that marks Allen's use of Mendelssohn's music indicates Allen's overall treatment of his predecessor, an indication perhaps of the extent to which he has intended to turn things upside down. *A Midsummer Night's Sex Comedy* is both homage and parody. Early in the movie, in the first 'country' scene, Andrew tries to fly on gauzy wings that recall Reinhardt's fairies. Later it turns out he can fly, not as a fairy but as a mechanical, on a sort of flying bicycle. As self-described 'crackpot inventor', Andrew makes the spirit ball that projects the 'unseen world' of 'ectoplasm and energies'. The humans are themselves the fairy element, as Leopold's eventual transformation indicates.

Reinhardt's famous sequence of the forest awakening to the music of the Scherzo helps Allen to make just this point. Reinhardt opens with a static, painted moon which at first appears full but which is, in fact, old and cradling its slightly darker complement. Beneath it is a painted forest. The sequence cuts to the contrastingly 'real' trees, using a descending shot to bring us from the heavens to earth. Then follows a series of shots of the forest twinkling with dew, a rising wind, and a series of animals (deer, owl, frogs, more deer). A brook runs through the wood. From the forest floor, Puck arises to howl at the moon and awaken the rest of the forest. A unicorn wanders through. The forest mist becomes a band of fairies, who spiral into the sky. Repeated cuts ensure the association of the moon and forest with the fairy world.

Allen plays with Reinhardt's sequence. His moon is full (as is Bergman's), seen through passing cloud, with the sound of frogs and crickets in the background. The spirit ball begins to rotate and glow as if in response to the moonshine. The music of a scherzo rises (not, as in Reinhardt, the scherzo of *A Midsummer Night's Dream*, but rather that of the 'Scottish' symphony). There follows a series of shots in rising light of woods, meadows, a pond with water lilies. As the light becomes brighter, the images become clearer, and we see flowers, a brook, various animals (a rabbit, a woodchuck, a marsh hen, a box turtle, a lady bug, a bee, a butterfly on flowers, a skunk, a pair of doves, finally a bounding deer); and, finally, Adrian arranging wildflowers at the kitchen table. Reinhardt is reversed and exaggerated. His forest awakening to moonlight is now a wood awakening to the dawn, his forest animated by fairies now full of animals, comically multiplied and humorously juxtaposed. And Reinhardt's careful association of the moon and forest with the fairies has been domesticated and humanized: Adrian arranges the flowers as a table decoration.

As if to clinch the point that he is concerned with the human and not the fairy world, Allen gives us no fairy dance in the wood, but rather a long sequence of his human characters at play in woods and meadows, wading in the brook, playing catch, fishing, catching butterflies, taking pictures, and so on. The same wood is later the scene of their mistimed meetings, nocturnal wanderings, and professions of love. Allen's wood is 'enchanted,' but it is enchanted with human spirits.

Allen deals similarly with Reinhardt's moon. Perhaps a vestige of stage scenery, the moon in the earlier film is always static and old. Even in the mechanicals' play, where moonshine wears a moon-shaped hat, the moon is on the wane. But it never actually wanes: there is no sense of movement. Allen, too adopts the moon as a central image, but he domesticates it. His moon is full, and remains so, perhaps as a sign of lunacy. But he also integrates this lunar roundness into a image pattern that pervades the film: Andrew's round goggles and glasses, the spirit ball and its projections, round picture frames and mirrors throughout the house, Andrew's flying machine, the telescope (which gives us the momentary, limited perspectives of Maxwell and, later, Leopold), and finally Leopold's spherical 'essence'.

The transformation of Leopold at the height of ecstasy emphasizes one of the film's central themes: the importance of the momentary and the immediate in a world that, like the moon, is bound to change. Maxwell is a master of the passionate moment, as his experience with Adrian has shown. This quality is the sum of his appeal to Ariel: 'I am the man of the moment.' Hence the many questions throughout the film about the relation of love and lust. The film glorifies the momentary and the transient, but argues that these allow a glimpse of the eternal. In a sort of epiphany, Maxwell loves Ariel at first smell, recognizing that she wears 'Blue Moonglow' perfume. Such moments promise transcendence. Leopold's metamorphosis at the 'highest moment of ecstasy' is an ekstasis, as his essence leaves his body and joins the other spirits in a now genuinely enchanted wood.

This theme of passionate immediacy is merely a corollary, however, to the impossibility of recapturing the past, a theme announced with the return of Ariel to Andrew's country house, the scene of her earlier brief, intense, but unconsummated affair with Andrew. Both characters feel the inadequacy of their current attachments, both regret their missed opportunity, and both sense, as Andrew explains to Maxwell, that their eventual union is somehow 'inevitable'. They walk together into the enchanted woods, reminiscing. They are under same tree, the same stars (the constellation Gemini is in the same place), the same moon, by the same brook. Ariel is even wearing the same dress. But their lovemaking – their attempt to reclaim their past in the present – is a disaster. Things that would never have bothered them years ago are now serious annoyances. In effect, they find themselves in a wood like Hall's, full of distracting noises and discomforts that no sense of missed opportunity can overcome. Nostalgia fails not because it is an inadequate motive for acting, but because it is insufficient to carry the act through to satisfactory completion.

The Camera as Spirit Ball

The woodsy scene of Ariel's and Andrew's failed romance is reminiscent for the film's audience as well as for its characters. It's what Maxwell's spirit ball, which shows 'the unseen world', has projected for the house guests a few minutes earlier. At least it is one possibility of that image, for each character has seen a projection of his or her own concerns. (Maxwell, for example, has seen his affair with Adrian.) The characters agree that they are seeing a missed opportunity, and they wonder if they are seeing the past or future. The subsequent events of the film make it clear that they and we are seeing both, that past and future overlie each other as a function of memory. Hence the central danger of unchecked nostalgia: the past threatens to distort the present and future.

For Allen, the lessons that the past cannot be recaptured (as for Ariel and Adrian) and that the momentary is therefore of crucial importance (as for Leopold) are more than just anti-nostalgic. They indicate Allen's unreverential, almost utilitarian attitude toward his filmic forebears. Allen makes his point with the spirit ball, an obvious metaphor for his own medium, which is itself a projection. Introducing this invention explicitly thematizes filmmaking in a context that demands attention to the past and the future of the art. Andrew speaks for Allen and his camera when he says of the spirit ball, 'I want that thing to emit light rays and capture the future and the past.'

Like the spirit ball, the camera captures the future and the past in the present. For Allen, film is the medium of the moment, and so it is the proper medium of our *Dreams*. Thus his film refuses merely to recapitulate past films or the theater history that lay distantly behind them, though it will unabashedly make use of this material. While acknowledging with his allusions the shaping influences of Shakespeare, Freud, Reinhardt, Bergman, and Hall, Allen still insists on his own independence. To a great extent, Allen seems to be taking the advice offered by Reinhardt a half-century earlier and since echoed by critics and filmmakers alike: 'The film must create its own new adequate mode of expression. It must open up new springs of composition, performance and music, must live on its own soil, without borrowing everywhere else. It must stand on its own foundation, so that it can dispense entirely with the photographed word.' Allen recognizes that his own accomplishment depends upon the 'foundation' – the mature and confident medium – that Reinhardt anticipates and helps to establish. It is thus fitting that when Leopold's 'pure essence' leaves the spirit ball (something that can only happen on film), Allen sends him out to join other spirits in the kind of forest Reinhardt envisioned: 'The woods are enchanted, filled with the spirits of the lucky men and women of passion who have passed away at the height of lovemaking.' And in a culminating gesture, Allen has Leopold deliver a Puckish epilogue that projects past cinematic enchantments into future *Dreams*: 'Promise me, all of you, to look for my glowing presence on starlit evenings in these woods under the summer moon.'

Notes

1. Max Reinhardt, 'On the Film', in *Max Reinhardt and His Theatre*, ed. Oliver M. Sayler, trans. Mariele S. Gundernatsch *et al.* (New York: Brentano's, 1926), pp. 62-64.
2. See John Collick, *Shakespeare, Cinema and Society* (Manchester: Manchester Univ. Press, 1989), pp. 80-93; Nick Roddick, *A New Deal in Entertainment: Warner Brothers in the 1930s* (London: British Film Institute, 1983), pp. 23, 231-33; and Roger Manvell, *Shakespeare and the Film* (South Brunswick and New York: A. S. Barnes, 1979), pp. 25-27.
3. The two directors divided their work in predictable fashion, Reinhardt being 'concerned with dialogue and leading the actors, and [Dieterle with] ... all technicalities connected with the filming' (Manvell, p. 25).
4. Rudolf Kommer, 'The Magician of Leopoldskron', in *Max Reinhardt and His Theatre*, ed. Oliver M. Sayler (New York: Brentano's, 1924), p. 12. This volume contains color plates of Ree's designs for Puck (opp. p. 36) and Oberon (opp. p. 38).
5. On Ree and Grot, see Elliot Stein, 'Filmographies of Art Directors and Production Designers', in Leon Barsacq, *Caligari's Cabinet and Other Grand Illusions: A History of*

Film Design, rev. and ed. Elliott Stein, trans. Michael Bullock (New York: New American Library, 1976), pp. 211-12, 236.

6. Andrew Bergman, *James Cagney*, Pyramid Illustrated History of the Movies (New York: Pyramid, 1973), quotes Reinhardt as saying that Cagney was 'the best actor in Hollywood ... few artists have ever had his intensity, his dramatic drive. Every movement of his body, and his incredible hands, contributes to the story he is trying to tell' (p. 60). Bergman does not cite his source.

7. Manvell, p. 26; Roddick, pp. 23, 231.

8. *A Midsummer Night's Dream*, foreword by Max Reinhardt (New York: Grosset & Dunlap, 1935). The quotation is from the front cover of the book jacket.

9. Allarydice Nicoll, *Film and Theatre* (New York: Thomas Crowell, 1936), pp. 175-81. Rpt. as 'Film Reality: Cinema and the Theatre', in *Focus on Shakespearean Films*, ed. Charles W. Eckert (Englewood Cliffs, NJ: Prentice-Hall, 1972), pp. 43-47.

10. Richard Watts, Jr., 'Films of a Moonstruck World', *The Yale Review* 25, no. 2 (Dec 1935), pp. 311-20. Rpt. in *Focus on Shakespearean Films*, ed. Charles W. Eckert (Englewood Cliffs, NJ: Prentice-Hall, 1972), p. 47. Otis Ferguson, 'Shakespeare in Hollywood' (16 October 1935), in *The Film Criticism of Otis Ferguson*, ed. Robert Wilson (Philadelphia: Temple University Press, 1971), pp. 97-98.

11. John Alfred Thomas, 'Shakespeare a la Cinema' (November 1935), in *From Quasimodo to Scarlett O'Hara: A National Board of Review Anthology 1920-1940*, ed. Stanley Hochman (New York: Frederick Ungar, 1982), p. 208.

12. Graham Greene, 'A Midsummer Night's Dream' (*The Spectator*, October 1935), in *The Pleasure Dome: The Collected Film Criticism 1935-40*, ed. John Russell Taylor (Oxford: Oxford University Press, 1980), pp. 28-29.

13. Quoted by Manvell, p. 123. Subsequent references to the comments of Peter Hall are to Manvell's volume and are cited parenthetically in the text. Manvell (p. 127) takes up the differences from Reinhardt's version, as does Michael Mullin, 'Peter Hall's Midsummer Night's Dream on Film', *Educational Theatre Journal*, 27 (1975), pp. 529-34.

14. See Jack J. Jorgens' appreciation of the film in his *Shakespeare on Film* (Bloomington: Indiana University Press, 1977), pp. 51-65.

15. See, for example, Robert Ornstein, 'Interpreting Shakespeare: The Dramatic Text and the Film', *The University of Dayton Review*, 14, no. 1 (1979-80), pp. 55-61.

16. See Vlada Petric, ed., *Films and Dreams: An Approach to Bergman* (South Salem, NY: Redgrave, 1981).

17. See Frank Gado, *The Passion of Ingmar Bergman* (Durham, NC: Duke University Press, 1986), pp. 21-22.

18. Stanley Cavell, *The World Viewed: Reflections on the Ontology of Film*, enlarged ed. (Cambridge, MA: Harvard, 1979), p. 50.

Welles's *Macbeth,* a Textual Parable

Bernice W. Kliman

Orson Welles burst into films before he was twenty-five, in 1941, with *Citizen Kane* – a work generally featured on everybody's list of the ten best films of all time. In spite of instant acclaim both for acting and directing, Welles had difficulty negotiating his way through the Hollywood establishment, and his attempts to retain artistic control over his work were often unsuccessful. His early attachment to Shakespeare made inevitable his films based on *Macbeth*, *Othello*, and *Henry the Fourth* (the last known as *Falstaff* or *Chimes at Midnight*), but he was able to film only the first within the United States. While the latter two films, released in 1952 and 1966, respectively, have earned a high place among Shakespeare films, the *Macbeth* has had a more troubled reception. Tracing its history clarifies Welles's relations with Hollywood and yields a parable that can apply to the production of any theatrical or film text.

Welles's *Macbeth* illustrates the complex interactions and artistic struggles that shape a production. The film, a Mercury Production, was a collaborative effort. A multi-faceted company, Mercury Productions was organized by John Houston and Orson Welles after they left the United States Government's Works Project Administration (W.P.A.), Federal Theater Project, where they had worked on the so-called 'Voodoo *Macbeth*', produced in Harlem in 1936.[1] Their first Mercury Theatre production was the 1937 *Julius Caesar* in modern dress, set in fascist Italy. Mercury Productions' several sub-groups worked on school editions, audio recordings, radio and stage shows, films, and the like. Though collaborative and organic processes led to a *Macbeth* different in some ways from Orson Welles's original idea, these were natural and beneficial features of his Mercury filmmaking. The Studio, with its narrow motives, inevitably affected the outcome also. Charles K. Feldman (Charlie), the Republic Pictures producer, for example, seemed to think that Lady Macbeth should be more like a Hollywood star than a Shakespearean character. He complains that 'The first scene of Lady Macbeth should be cut in my opinion because I think she looks horrible and frightening, and everyone who has seen the picture ...

was appalled at the looks of the girl. In her next scene she looks infinitely better – as a matter of fact she looks damned attractive.... The soliloquy we lose may be of some importance, but I think it is of greater importance to have the right opening for the girl'.[2] Finally the reviewers and the first audiences had their say. Over a period of several years, Welles attempted to make the film a marketable as well as artistic commodity, but eventually his new film, *Othello*, diminished his interest in the *Macbeth* film, and he let it go to make its own way.

The story of the film's evolution is available because one of his Mercury collaborators, Richard Alan Wilson, saved almost every scrap of paper – scripts at every stage of development, memos, voice recordings, letters, reviews, and drawings – and, at the end of a long Hollywood career, deposited them in the Special Collection Library at the University of California at Los Angeles. Breezily affectionate in his letters, Welles salutes Wilson as 'my dearest partner of greatness'. Wilson was Welles's right-hand man, who, as associate producer, was a constant go-between for Welles, the rest of the production crew and the studio brass. Difficulties abounded, and the Wilson material, including his own comments and explanations, details the struggle. While the memos sketch the sociology of collaborative filmmaking, the scripts record the traces of that interaction.[3]

As is well known, Welles designed the film to buoy up filmed Shakespeare, which clunkers like the 1930s *As You Like It* and *Romeo and Juliet* had virtually sunk – fond as many Shakespeare fans are of these films. Intense preparation would, Welles thought, enable his team to create a low budget yet artistic film and make Shakespeare an attractive product. Trying in March 1947 to sell British producer Alexander Korda the film, Welles said he could have a script ready in three weeks, that he was ready to drop everything and come to London to talk about casting: 'Can start Macbeth instant costumes ready shoot fast because much detailed work already put into production plan' (box 25). After Korda refused the offer, Republic Pictures, known for its low-budget films, came through, hoping perhaps to change its image. With the film in their sights, the cast rehearsed the script thoroughly for Mercury's ANTA (American National Theater and Academy) production in Salt Lake City at the Utah Centennial Festival, ending June 1947. As several scholars, including Andrea Nouryeh, have shown,[4] Welles didn't distinguish greatly between stage and screen texts: in both media he reshaped, transposed, and sliced long scenes into fragments to further his creative aims. Thus the ANTA text and the practice on stage would speed the filmmaking. A film production's main expense is camera time; Welles planned to get this film into the can in twenty-two days, achieving a B-picture budget of $700,000 by scripting with Hitchcock-like attention to sequences, filming schedules, setting, and style. The actual camera time, according to the record of dailies (the shots completed each day), was twenty-three days, from Friday, June 20 to Thursday, July 17, 1947.

What should have been a *tour de force* and the harbinger of many other Hollywood Shakespeare films directed by Welles was instead a disaster – not so much in filmmaking as in postproduction, marketing and packaging. After mixed previews and reviews in 1947-48, largely because the film did not reach its ideal audience and because showings were continuous rather than scheduled, the heads of Republic Pictures in December 1948 yanked the 106- or 107-minute film. They insisted on pruning to speed the pace and on relooping (rerecording) the sound track to eliminate the Scottish burr, which they thought unintelligible. The pruning worked better than the relooping. With Welles in Europe trying to make *Othello*, yet insisting on artistic control, the project dragged on, reopening in March 1950 at a spare 86 minutes; but still success eluded the project. Memories of the first release tantalized film buffs. In 1979, UCLA's Bob Gitt with the help of the Folger Shakespeare Library and the National Endowment for the Arts restored the original film, by reintroducing cut scenes and adding an original voice track (while retaining the Jacques Ibert music composed for the rerelease). This version became available on videotape several years ago. Perfectly intelligible, it seems to many who have seen both films an improvement over the rerelease. Thus, there are three films, each highlighting different facets of collaboration: the original release (1947), which, with several significant differences, is close to the restoration (1979), and the rerelease (1950), the response to the film's initial poor showing.[5]

One script in the Wilson collection captures the film as originally shot, with one numbered scene for each camera setup, a total of 645 shots. Labeled a cutting continuity, this postproduction script (or one like it) plus the outtakes (that is, the excised frames) must have given Gitt the information he needed to restore the original from the rerelease, which had no more than 547 shots. With the shots to be pruned marked in grease pencil, the longer script contains two layers: the film as completed and the film after compressing 12 reels into 9: it is thus a double script. The most interesting script to compare to this late double script is the earliest, dated May 16, 1947 and written by Welles himself, with 41 scenes not broken yet into separate camera setups. Wilson notes the rarity of such scripts; more often, a filmmaker will convey the overall plan orally or through a story summary to studio script writers. Welles explicitly names the emotional content he seeks while clarifying for Republic Pictures personnel, bewildered by the poetic settings, how the filming would work.[6] As an intermediate phase between the ANTA stage script and the true shooting script, for which the studio staff divided the scenes into shots, the early script marks Welles's turn from stage thinking to screen thinking.

Though he had the whole film in his mind at the beginning, Welles was a tinkerer and thus responsive to the idea of change. Therefore it is wrong to assume that any deviation from his first-released film is bad. Change is a constant – from first concept through first filming through final editing of the rereleased film. Even during his first filming, if a good idea occurred to him, to one of the actors, or to one of his staff, very likely Welles would use it; unbelievably, his short schedule was supple enough to accommodate these shifts. Many items from the Wilson Collection document the changes. In the days before word processors or photo-copying machines, the studio and Wilson systematically coded revisions by using, successively, white, blue, pink, yellow, and green sheets. Some scripts in the collection are a kaleidoscope of colors. A prayer in Latin and English on a white sheet is replaced later by a Celtic prayer, when the studio's research department finds one (box 11, f.8). The shots of Cawdor being dragged in and placed on the executioner's block are recorded on a green sheet, signaling that his presence was a late addition. Amazingly, many of the film's most memorable sequences are added to the early script. The image of Seyton hanging from the bell rope was late, as was Lady Macbeth's suicidal leap into an endless crevasse, a special effect that cost $53.36 when redone for the rerelease (invoice, 27 February 1950, box 12, f.5). Also, the crown (that falls from the beheaded doll of Macbeth) in Fleance's hands, his eyes turned angelically upward, is another late addition (recorded in dailies as shot 91). Welles's concept of the friar, a character who derives partly from Ross, partly from an entirely new, non-Shakespearean idea, developed during the filmmaking. Beginning as Holy Father, he became for Welles more ambiguous. Memos show Wilson struggling with Welles about changing the character late in the day: 'Lou [Lindsay, the editor] also told me of your desire to change Alan Napier's character from a Holy Father to something else.... Let's have an answer on this....' Even though the credits in the restored film call him 'Holy Father', he is a much seedier character than he appears to be in the initial script. Change, then, is to be expected in a Welles project – along with a fundamental vision that remains consistent in all the *Macbeth* projects, from the Harlem 'Voodoo' production (1936) through the rereleased film (1950).

Sometimes his cuts were inspired. Welles eliminates from his first script a sentimental scene in which Macbeth, having taken part in the murder of the Macduff family, carries a dead boy to his throne and strokes his head. He wanted Macbeth to be, in essence, a noble person, but this mourning scene would have strained credibility. The drastic cutting for the rerelease of Macbeth's entire scene suborning the murderers works surprisingly well; the film dissolves smoothly from Banquo's leavetaking to the two murderers ready to ambush him and Fleance (from shot 284 directly to shot 332). More problematically, the studio also forced Welles to cut parts of Macbeth's soliloquy expressing his doubts about killing Duncan (I.3.134-37; I.7.21-25), but he successfully resisted other cuts from his soliloquies, keeping, for example, the first part of 'If it were done' through 'We'd jump the life to come' (I.7.1-7). Wilson expresses Welles's view in a memo to Robert Newman and another studio executive, Herbert Yates. After justifying each of the soliloquies leading to the murder, Wilson says, 'Any further cutting ... would bring Shakespeare's audiences more seriously on our heads and would definitely jeopardize Macbeth as a tragic character.' Without many words or deeds to help the audience, expression alone often had to communicate Macbeth's nobility. That Welles succeeds in conveying the subtext without text to support it is a credit to his acting ability. Throughout his career, limitations brought out his best solutions.

No one aspect of the film gave more trouble than the supernatural, and no other aspect better demonstrates Welles's evolving concepts and concessions to exigencies. The witches of the originally released film disturbed the producers almost as much as had the Scottish accent. With their exaggerated witchiness, they were, Republic thought, more silly than frightening. But Welles, too, was not completely satisfied with them; when the three actors could not actualize his conception, he was forced to reshape their scenes.

The early script interjects the witches repeatedly, for example, before Lady Macbeth and Macbeth meet to discuss the arrival of Duncan – with Hecate's lines from III.5 – and just before the appearance of the dagger (II.1) – with lines from I.3. Welles moves, from early script to final creation, towards greater simplicity, leaving more to the viewer's imagination. With each succeeding script, he recedes further from his design for the Voodoo *Macbeth*, in which the witches and their cohorts were a dominant feature, appearing in six scenes of eight, particularly at the ends of scenes, as visual and aural punctuation.[7] Though the film compared to the Harlem production plays down their overriding control over events, it similarly punctuates important scenes. In both the early script and the postproduction script before pruning, the witches reappear after Macbeth exits with Ross, the friar and Banquo, and share lines 30-31 from Hecate's speech in the normally excised III.5. In the postproduction script:

[shot] 73.   'MED. CLOSE UPWARD ANGLE (MIST)'
on the Three, shooting over rocky formation.
THE FIRST:
He shall spurn fate.

THE SECOND:
Scorn death.

THE THIRD:
And bear his hopes above wisdom!

THE FIRST:
Grace!

74.   MED. LONG DOWN ANGLE (MIST)
On group as Macbeth Mounts.
THE SECOND: O.S. [i.e., voiceover]
And fear!

Welles had amplified the witches even more in his early script for the film, where a few lines from the witches' Sabbath precede the same lines from III.5: Welles writes, 'The three witches crawl out of their hiding place, and the first leads the others in the weaving of a spell....' that includes the 'thrice to thine' lines (I.3.35-36). At the conclusion, 'They smile at each other.' The rerelease eliminates their lines after Macbeth's exit and simply ends the scene with a ghostly 'Hail!' on the fadeout.

Another punctuating shot in all three film scripts, after Banquo's exit from the court, shows the three with their forked sticks, the castle in the background, then, in a dissolve, a small Macbeth doll, moisture running down its face. As a witch says lines that in the text do not apply to Macbeth ('I will drain him dry as hay.... He shall live a man forbid' from I.3.18-22), a hand reaches into the frame and claps the crown on the doll's head, its face now distorted into a sneer. The image dissolves into that of Macbeth, staring into his distorted reflection in a metal mirror before the banquet scene, his face beaded with sweat. Also, when Macduff jeers 'untimely ripp'd' in response to Macbeth's boast that no man born of woman will harm him, Welles again introduces a shot of the three and has them echo Macduff's words. The early script has Macbeth see them through a window; in the films they are simply *there*. Similarly, while the cauldron scene is their last in the play, the post-production script calls not only for a long shot of the witches, with their 'forked sticks, silhouetted against the mist', to end the film, but also for a final shot, a superimposition of (that is, a dissolve to) a close-medium shot of the same image. The First Witch says at the end, just as in the Harlem production, 'Peace!/ The charm's wound up.' The early script has a similar ending, but even more overtly stresses the witches' control:

41   **A CORNER OF THE CASTLE.**

> The three weird sisters appear on the scene. The Second Witch opens her mouth to speak. The First stops her with a complacent gesture of her skinny hand.

>> FIRST WITCH
>> Peace!
>> The charm's wound up.

> Overscene there continues the scirling bagpipes, the mighty shouts of the crowd. – We read the end of the story in the Witch's eyes.
>> FADEOUT.

THE END

The double script shows the last line deleted for the rerelease. In an eight-page memo to Wilson that describes alternatives for the last shot, Welles writing from the set of *Othello* knows that he cannot control the witches' performance.

After several detailed suggestions for visual and sound effects, he states, and he underlines,

I think we should try a fadeout without the witches closing line.

In this version we would do without the close shot of the witches. We would bring in the tomorrow and tomorrow clouds at the same musical place during the pull back. and then immediately before the pull-back action is completed ... the clouds take over from the pull-back-castle image. Then the clouds slowly fadeout but in this version definately not before THE END has faded in. In this version THE END and the clouds will fadeout together, just as the music proper finishes, There will be a grand Mercury pause over a black screen (perhaps with very low tympani keeping the screen alive) and then the Republic trademark will slowly slowly slowly fadein and hold for the length of the closing distant fanfare.

I have high hopes for this version.

The witches may stink it up – I hope not, but they may.

The Gitt restoration, in other words, because it includes the last line from the originally-released film and the medium shot of the witches, does not represent Welles's last thoughts about the scene – does not respond to Welles's concern that they may 'stink it up'. The omission of the last shot is just one example of the rerelease improving, in Welles's mind, on the original. The extra year and a half gave him time to correct some aspects he hadn't liked. Since he had been willing to release the film originally with the witches' less-than-adequate performances, his film benefits from the studio's dislike of cackling witchiness, for though the rerelease cuts their lines, it enhances their menace. The rerelease and to a somewhat lesser extent the restoration solve the problem of retaining the witches' theatrical energy while not allowing them to swamp the production (as they did the Harlem version), but with its trimmed sound track, the rerelease better upholds their mystery. We must ascribe part of the solution to the studio's interference and part to Welles's ability to satisfy their demands creatively.

Welles's image of the witches' three main scenes – the first scene (I.1), their greeting of Macbeth (I.3), and the cauldron scene (IV.1) – also changes. His early script has a straightforward first scene, to which the postproduction script adds elements from the cauldron scene. Welles calls them in his early script 'wicked old women' and 'wise women', but they seem unlike women in the final film because, never shown clearly, they remain unknowable and otherworldly. In the film but not in the early script, they have the power to reach into the boiling cauldron, from which they bring to birth the doll they will use to control Macbeth. The figure is recognizably Macbeth, though none of the scripts note this resemblance (a memo of 11 February 1948 mentions creating a new figure; perhaps it was not until the rerelease, then, that the doll *did* resemble Welles). Structure is similar in the two scripts, for, in both, the first

31

scene merges into the third (the prophetic greeting of Macbeth and Banquo), interrupted only by the credits, without the bloody sergeant scene (I.2). The more intense rerelease is better without Gitt's restoration of several lines and images, particularly the lines from the cauldron scene (dialogue under shots of them reaching into the cauldron) and from Banquo's part. As cut for the rerelease, they work without speaking, and Banquo doesn't ask for his fate, the witches volunteering only the information that he will 'get kings Though thou be none'. In the early script the witches disappear before the entrance of Ross and the friar. In the later scripts, the friar warns them off, and they fall back before his staff. This power over them requires another change – his death at the end to assure their ascendancy.

In the film, the cauldron scene is the witches' only full scene after the opening sequence. The early script introduces it after a fadeout of the banquet scene. The scene, in the traditional cavern, opens with Macbeth's arrival:

> SECOND WITCH
> By the pricking of my thumbs,
> Something wicked this way comes.
>
> Macbeth enters the Cavern, followed by a bitter gust of wind.
>
> MACBETH
> How now, you secret, black, and midnight hags!
> What is't you do? (IV.1.45-46, 49-50).

After this initial greeting, the scene continues with the opening of IV.1, the brewing of the cauldron's foul mixture, which Macbeth observes, 'flattened against the slimy wall of the cave'. The dailies show that the witches were shot reflected in a mirror, their images distorted, while they spoke the prophecies, a visual echo of Macbeth's face in the distorted mirror before arranging Banquo's murder.

The double script merges the banquet and the cauldron scenes, with the cavernous tunnel of the one merging into the open wilderness of the other. Terrorized by drunken visions of Banquo (and then Duncan), Macbeth runs from the banquet directly to a promontory where he conjures the witches to speak to him, and, invisible throughout, they respond with the three prophecies. Beginning with a high angle long shot of a far distant Macbeth, his face lit by lightning flashes, the scene fades out on a high angle closeup of Macbeth speaking directly to the camera: 'But is all this so?' The answer comes, 'Aye. sir, all this is so', as the image fades to the Macduff scene. The witches have fewer lines in the film than in the early script and do not even appear on the screen, but their uncanny discovery on Macbeth's own ground heightens their eeriness. Since the actors playing the witches couldn't deliver what Welles or anyone else wanted, Welles, pressed by necessity, shaped them into a usable aural image.

For relooping the witches' least satisfactory lines, Welles secured the help of English actress Fay Compton, Emilia in his *Othello*, who, one memo says, was willing to spend a day on witch dialogue for the film, working with Welles in Europe, but it is not clear that she actually did the job. And though equipment and technicians followed him to Europe to elicit his approval and his personal dubbing of dialogue relooped in the United States, there was no substitute for being on the spot. Wilson couldn't always accomplish the task as Welles wanted. Welles, for example, writes to Wilson, unhappy with Jeanette Nolan's (Lady Macbeth's) new sound:

> Jean Nolan's Montana 'r' is excruciating, and will excite, without any question whatso-ever, a great deal of unfavourable comment, not only in England but also in all metro-politan areas of the English speaking world where ears are educated to these broad dis-tinctions of speech.
> Particularly unhappy is the change not only in speech, but actually in **character**.
> When Miss Nolan moves from the Scottish speech (**in which she had been rehearsed**) to what she considers a normal speech for Shakespeare, her vocal tone moves at least an octave upwards, and the entire personality of Lady Macbeth vanishes. We are given in-stead an intense and sometimes intelligent reading of the lines by an American farm girl. It would be impossible to state strongly enough the gravity of this mistake. Nolan is not a large woman; her personality is not commanding. She lacks what the French call 'pre-sence'. Her success in the role of Lady Macbeth was entirely based on her intelligence and on the vocal authority which informed and underlined the playing of all her big scenes. The unfortunate Montana whine, wheeze, and scrape completely nullify this authority. The result is downright embarrassing, and as the producer of the film I cannot permit this to be countenanced.

Disagreeing with Welles's earnest request that Nolan's lines not be redubbed, Wilson writes to Studio head Robert V. Newman that 85% of her lines *have* been relooped [and thus are ready for redubbing], all except the sleepwalking scene. 'We would never have enough time or money to follow the dictates of [Welles's] memo. I have, however, in added re-looping, eliminated to the best of her and my ability (consistent with cost and time considerations) this obj-ection [to her Montana accent]...'

In an earlier memo (November 18, 1948), Wilson explained the use of a Scottish accent:

> We didn't put a Scotch dialect in the picture because Macbeth was laid in Scotland. A Scotch dialect was put in because we determined, **after careful tests**, that the intelligibil-ity was greater with the Scotch accent, because it had a tendency to slow the actors down just enough to make it more comprehensible to the ear. The secondary reason was that it absolutely made it impossible for the actor to sing his lines ala Shakespearian declamation.

Though the idea was excellent, though the Scottish accent did help the actors to be less declamatory (just as the Caribbean accent similarly helped the cast of the Harlem *Macbeth*), Wilson did not succeed completely in carrying this point with the studio.

Welles kept on trying. In a memo of March 6, 1949, Welles writes to 'Dearest Charlie' [Feldman]:

> Although we only took 21 days for shooting the film, we spent – you may remember – many weeks of very hard work prerecording, and many more weeks of equally hard work dubbing and re-dubbing dialogue afterwards. This represents as much of my efforts as all the other parts of the picture put together, and to re-do this completely under anyone else's supervision (even Dick's [Richard Wilson], in whom I need not say I have the utmost confidence) would be to remove from the film more than fifty percent of my contribution to it.

Welles's assessment of the total time spent on the film is certainly accurate. In addition to all the preliminary preparation, including the ANTA work and the precording of dialogue, postproduction work on the film continued, according to memos, at least through November 1947 (box 10, f.6). Welles suggests that they 're-record all difficult and questioned parts of the film. '**But to re-do everything would be quite literally to undo everything.**' Since the burr remains in many lines, clearly Welles's advice was heeded. On the other hand, Wilson pleads that

> Attention [be paid] to the old problem of matching in terms of voice and volume levels, quality, acoustics, etc. It seems to me important that you remember that this is becoming more and more a patch up job and therefore, we should bend over backwards to do the work in the way that will minimize this patch up effort. By this, I mean if there is time, all the loops should be done and particularly all the loops of any given speech should be done because our problem is going to be intercutting lines within the same speech.

Welles himself, in checking the relooping, realized that the patching would not work and insisted that speeches be completely redone without the Scottish accent, instead of the word or two he had earlier proposed. 'Obviously,' he writes in a memo, 'if the Scots burr *was* to be taken out, **every single evidence of it should go**' (box 25). A Wilson memo to Robert V. Newman expresses the confusion:

> In [Welles's] memo, with sharpness and at length, he criticized the fact that if were to do any removal of the dialect he assumed we would do every bit. Yet he sent back loops undone which we requested, and left untouched of his own volition and without comment practically the whole latter part of the picture. He 'assumed' a 'thoroughness' when the policy decided upon was based on his own request and reasoning to the contrary (box 11, f.6).

Compromises eventually soothed the clashes of opinion and smoothed out the disparate goals. The sound of the rerelease compares favorably to the restored sound, and many of the cuts improve the film.

34

We have, then, pieces of a whole that we can puzzle out. Like a Shakespeare text, Welles's *Macbeth* requires some archeology to work out the accurate text. Or perhaps a better way to put it is that, like a Shakespeare text, and for the same reasons, there is no one, accurate text. Michael Goldman demonstrates through the example of *Hamlet*[8] that each script provides its own set of opportunities and responsibilities, that each provides an array of choices suitable for a particular moment.[9] When a work is the result of collaboration, when the process allows for continual change, no individual text can be selected as *the* correct version. Some of the changes are the result of Welles's revisions: should the 'true' film, then, be the one he himself superseded? Other changes are the result of interference for commercial reasons, but Welles ultimately accepted them. On November 14, 1949, he writes to his colleague Richard Alan Wilson:

> Dearest Dick... I am sorry you find yourself so much at odds with the final editing of 'Macbeth' as done by Lou [Lindsay] and myself. Your suggestions are always interesting and often impressive but I'm afraid this last version should stand as it is.... Republic-Feldman, Lindsay and Welles are generally content with this last form. There has been alot of disagreement up till now and it seems to me a shame to enperil this strange, pleasant, new atmosphere.... In my view our job on Macbeth is finished. Given limitless time, more money and a great deal of loving patience and passion on the part of Republic, we might continue to piddle and diddle around with it, but particularly since I am one whole ocean and a continent away from the scene of operations, it seems to me we had better address the damned thing, stamp it, and send it off to its destiny ... [sic, these ellipses are Welles's] whatever that may be.[10]

The film exists as a valid entity in every stage of its progress. Thanks to Richard Alan Wilson, the materials are available. The full story awaits telling.

Notes

All references are to Kenneth Muir, ed., *Macbeth*, Arden Shakespeare (London: Methuen, 1982).

1. See Bernice W. Kliman, 'Orson Welles's 1936 "Voodoo" *Macbeth* and its Reincarnation on Film', in *Macbeth*. Shakespeare in Performance Series (Manchester: University of Manchester Press, 1992), pp. 86-99.
2. All manuscript materials cited are from the Richard Alan Wilson Collection, UCLA (call no. 1154); the Feldman letter is dated May 10, 1949. I identify items, where possible, by date, box and/or folder number and retain original punctuation and spelling. My appreciation to the UCLA Special Collections Library staff for their assistance.
3. To summarize the main scripts: (1) Orson Welles's script with 41 scenes, May 16, 1947 (box 11, f.7); (2) the shooting script as marked up by Lou Lindsay, the editor, with 91 shots, June 16, 1947 (box 11, f.8); (3) another copy of this shooting script, heavily marked, with first and last pages missing, and with white and pink sheets, no date (box

11, f.9); (4) another copy of this shooting script with blue, pink, yellow, and green sheets, heavily marked by a script assistant; the color code indicates level of revision (box 11, f.10); (5) copies of sheets taken from scripts along with green sheets (box 11, f.9); (6) the record of the dailies showing the number of versions of each shot and Orson Welles's reactions to the rushes (box 10, f.5); (7) the cutting continuity with 645 shots, marked with cuts (box 10, f.2); (8) a copy of this cutting continuity (box 10, f.3); (9) an earlier version from which the cutting continuity was made, with an instruction sheet dated Sept. 1, 1949 noting that a blue squiggle through a word indicated that it required relooping to replace the Scottish 'dialect' (box 10, f.4); (10) a cutting continuity, 547 shots, with cuts executed mostly as marked on (7), labeled 'final', with narration substituted for some shots (box 10, f.7). Copies of several scripts have been deposited in the Folger Shakespeare Library.

4. Andrea Nouryeh, 'Understanding Xanadu: An Alternative Way of Viewing Orson Welles's Shakespeare Films', *Shakespeare on Film Newsletter* 14.1 (Dec. 1989), p. 3.

5. The Library of Congress has no version of the film. The Folger Shakespeare Library has the restored film, both on film and tape, the film beginning with 8 minutes of orchestral music by Jacques Ibert, who was, as memos reveal, a source of constant concern and difficulty during the preparation for rerelease. The Museum of Modern Art has both the restored and the rereleased film, and I am grateful to the Museum of Modern Art Film Department and its director Charles Silver for allowing me to screen the rereleased film. According to Kenneth S. Rothwell (Kenneth S. Rothwell and Annabelle Henkin Melzer, *Shakespeare on Screen: An International Filmography and Videography* (New York: Neal-Schumann, 1990), the film is available for rent both in rereleased and restored form. An opportunity to compare the original release to the rerelease and to the restored version could yield further insights, but no copy of the original has, apparently, survived.

6. The script with other Wilson materials provides full details: three cameras churned simultaneously and takes were long. Instead of repeating 'takes', Welles selected specific cuts from among the three sets of rushes, reshooting only when necessary. The dialogue, too, was prerecorded in several different styles in a sound studio so that the best could be used for the film's sound track. An innovation derived from filmed musicals, this way of composing the sound track would assure quality control, Welles thought. The actors performed while listening to their speeches. In an explanatory note, Wilson says that they shot 85 to 90% of the film in one large space with movable pillars, another 10% in a Republic set with tunnels and caverns left over from a serial. They shot only a few scenes outside on the back lot, enhancing them with matte shots.

7. See Richard France, ed., *Orson Welles on Shakespeare: The W.P.A. and Mercury Theatre Playscripts*. Contributions in Drama and Theatre Studies 30 (Westport, CT: Greenwood Press, 1990).

8. Michael Goldman, '*Hamlet*: Entering the Text', *Theatre Journal* 44 (1992), pp. 449-60.

9. Stephen Orgel, 'What is a Text?', *Research Opportunities in Renaissance Drama* 24 (1981), pp. 3-6.

10. Welles possibly could feel satisfied at this point because he had gotten his way about several scenes. The studio had objected, for example, to shots of the Macduff child (played by Welles's daughter) running and falling, yet these remain. They had also denied the effectiveness of a high angle extreme long shot, a shot that Welles had

sketched – a rarity in the collection – of Macbeth standing, staff in hand, on a snow-covered courtyard, but the shot appears after the 'I 'gin to be a-weary of the sun' soliloquy in the rereleased film (shot 510; V.5.49).

The 'Bloody Business' of Roman Polanski's *Macbeth*: A Case Study of the Dynamics of Modern Shakespeare Appropriation

Per Serritslev Petersen

It is the bloody business which informs/ Thus to mine eyes.

– *Macbeth* II.1.47-8[1]

It is a disquieting thought that the major part of the commentaries on Shakespeare's passions and his politics are hatched far from life by sheltered figures behind ivy-covered halls. [...] Our greatest problem in England where we have the best possibility in the world for presenting our greatest author is just this – the relating of these works to our lives. [...] It is Poland that in our time has come closest to the tumult, the danger, the intensity, the imaginativeness and the daily involvement with the political process that made life so horrible, subtle and ecstatic to an Elizabethan. So it is quite naturally up to a Pole to point us the way.

– Peter Brook's preface to Jan Kott's *Shakespeare Our Contemporary*[2]

A production of *Macbeth* not evoking a picture of the world flooded with blood would inevitably be false.

– Jan Kott's *Shakespeare Our Contemporary*[3]

Macbeth contained only a fraction of the gore that characterizes any Peckinpah movie, but the violence was realistic. *Macbeth* is a violent play, and I've never believed in cop-outs.

– Roman Polanski's *Roman*[4]

The Pole that Peter Brook, the English Shakespeare director *par excellence* of the fifties and sixties, claimed could 'point us the way', was not, of course,

Roman Polanski. It was Jan Kott, drama professor at the University of Warsaw and author of a book which Brook himself contributed to making a best-seller in the progressive academe of the swinging sixties, viz. *Shakespeare Our Contemporary* (1965). Despite his reputation as 'the last authentic *enfant terrible* of [English] stagecraft',[5] Brook would hardly have thought of associating the then London-based international film director Roman Polanski with his 'Contemporary-Shakespeare movement', even though it could be argued that Polanski's *Polish* background was considerably more dramatic (and traumatic) than Kott's, in terms of personal closeness to what Brook describes as 'the tumult, the danger, the intensity, the imaginativeness and the daily involvement with the political process that made life so horrible, subtle and ecstatic to the Elizabethan'. But then Polanski belonged to 'that young directorial talent' that had gone 'straight into TV and cinema, bypassing the theatre altogether':[6] within the English cultural scene of the mid-sixties, Polanski's uniquely Polish – *and* Jewish – background was channelled exclusively into the Cinema, as distinct from the Theatre, of the Absurd and of Cruelty – witness movies like *Repulsion* (1965), *Cul-de-Sac* (1966), and *Dance of the Vampires* (1967). These films can be seen to articulate Polanski's Polish-Jewish *vision du monde*, his nihilistic 'faith in the absurd' (*Roman* 392), embodying both his memories of the Nazi Holocaust and of the postwar Stalinist regime, which he had 'fought with mockery in Poland's real-life theater of the absurd' (*Roman* 393).

Polanski's *Macbeth* film was made in England in 1970 and premiered in New York in January 1971. But in order to appreciate the highly complex and confused nature of the psychobiographical and sociocultural dynamics that determined, first, Polanski's own reception/appropriation/adaptation of Shakespeare's tragedy, and, second, the subsequent critical reception(s) of the film, we need to explore, in some detail, not only the director's Polish-Jewish hinterland and life/career on the Western side of the Iron Curtain (including some – cinematically as well as existentially – significant events that occurred during the three or four years that separated *Dance of the Vampires* and *Macbeth*), but also the time-honoured conventions of Shakespeare bardolatry along with the condition of modern Western theatre in general.

As E. Pearlman notes in his analysis of the politics of Polanski's *Macbeth*, the view of the world represented in the film is 'remarkably pessimistic' and 'antithetical in almost all respects to Shakespeare's'.[7] In the happy ending of Shakespeare's play, 'the time is free' again after 'th'usurper's cursed head' has been lopped off: law and order, that is, the semi-divine monarchy of Scotland, will now be restored in its proper 'measure, time, and place' by the legitimate heir to the throne, the 'most sainted' King Duncan's equally sainted son Malcolm, still 'unknown to woman' (IV.3.111, 126). In Polanski's film version (the script and scenario of which were the result of six weeks' intensive collaboration with the theatre critic Kenneth Tynan in London), Shakespeare's happy ending has been radically undercut in order to reinforce Polanski's own philosophical message of nihilism and absurdism. Let me list the most significant alterations, revisions, deletions, and additions, which have a direct bearing on Polanski's 'tragic' ending.

Malcolm's 'measure, time, and place' speech that concludes Shakespeare's *Macbeth* has been cut in its entirety. Instead we focus once more on the usurper's cursed head, now carried along on its pole. But then, imperceptibly almost, the visual perspective is shifted from Malcolm's victorious, jubilant army to Macbeth's still open eyes (who would have bothered to close them anyway?), and, in a kind of surreal after-image or out-of-body experience, we share Macbeth's nightmare experience – on top of the pole – of being 'baited with the rabble's curse', 'the show and gaze o'th'time' (V.8.29, 24). A typically ingenious and macabre Polanskian-cinema *tour de force*. From the outset, Polanski realized that not only could Shakespeare's play not be turned into a film without extensive cuts, but 'many scenes would have to be kaleidoscoped into a visual whole' (*Roman* 291). So this deletion/revision is not just a gratuitous cinematic gimmick: the dramatic and thematic significance of the new ending is, of course, to ensure that the audience is, as it were, stuck with the existential tragedy of Macbeth, even beyond his death and to the point of total emotional and visual empathy, if not sympathy. And, by the same token, the audience is deprived of the 'comic relief' provided by Malcolm's happy ending, 'by the grace of Grace'.

In Polanski's *Macbeth,* Malcolm's 'Grace' would have been of questionable value anyway, thanks to the character of Rosse. In Shakespeare's *dramatis personae*, Rosse belongs to the rather shadowy group of 'noblemen of Scotland' serving the King, but in Polanski's screenplay he gets promoted to the dramatic and thematic status of Machiavellian archvillain, a corrupt opportunist and survivor in the dirty game of power politics. He manages to serve three royal masters: first Duncan, then Macbeth, and last Malcolm, to whom he presents the crown, after Macbeth's decapitation, with the words (Macduff's line in Shakespeare's play): 'Hail, King of Scotland.' Thus, from the very start, Malcolm's reign is seen to be morally and politically tainted with the corruption of the man that has served Macbeth as his number-one henchman. In Polanski's version, Rosse has not only performed as Shakespeare's anonymous Third Murderer in the liquidation of Banquo; he has also masterminded the massacre of the Macduff household. At the opportune moment, Rosse changes sides once more and joins Malcolm's army in England. When, in the final showdown, Macbeth hurls his battleaxe away in disgust, it glances off Rosse's headpiece, removing it and unmasking the turncoat. This peripheral incident in the film flow also illustrates Polanski's resourcefulness in ways of 'kaleidoscoping' thematic issues into cinematic images, in this case Macbeth's tragic awareness that he should not look to have 'honour, love, obedience, troops of friends' (V.3.25).

In Polanski's version, Macbeth nobly spares Macduff's life, at one point, in their long, elaborately choreographed combat, uttering the lines 'my soul is too much charg'd/ With blood of thine already' (V.8.5-6). Thus Polanski again tries to tip the scales in favour of Macbeth as tragic-existential hero (making demands on our human empathy) as distinct from the demonic 'Hell-hound' denounced by Malcolm, Macduff *et hoc genus*. In *Roman Polanski*, Paul Werner is clearly confusing the Shakespearean and Polanskian tragedies (and philosophies) when he argues that Macbeth's death has 'nichts Heroisches an sich': 'er weigert sich anfangs sogar, sich dem Zweikampf, Mann gegen Mann, zu stellen [*sic*] – Stolz und Würde haben für ihn schon längst keine Bedeutung mehr'.[8]

Act V of Shakespeare's *Macbeth* comprised nine scenes. Polanski, however, has added a tenth scene, a kind of epilogue corresponding to the opening pre-credits prologue (to which I shall return in due course). In this scene, music-ally accompanied by the demonic cacophony of the previous witches' scenes, we see Malcolm's younger brother Donalbain wending his way, on horseback, through the bleak Scottish wilderness, his destination being the underground cavern of the Weird Sisters. Macbeth the usurper has also found *his* successor: in Polanski's Manichean universe, the evil empire is bound to strike back, re-peating the vicious circle again and again. From Act I Donalbain has been de-monized in the screenplay, physically stigmatized through an awkward limp and an ugly scowl, so we naturally suspect this character of some evil poten-tial, say, the wickedness of a Richard III, another demonic Shakespearean limper. In Act I, Malcolm, as Duncan's eldest son, is officially declared suc-cessor to the throne ('Prince of Cumberberland'), and Macbeth and Donalbain are both seen to respond to this royal announcement by scowling their extreme displeasure (in Macbeth's case, supplemented, of course, with the Shakespear-ean aside: 'The Prince of Cumberland! – That is a step/ On which I must fall down, or else o'erleap,/ For in my way it lies' (I.4.47-50)). So it is no surprise that Donalbain, when returning from Ireland to liberated Scotland, refuses to take part in his brother Malcolm's 'gracious' celebration of the victory, but is *anderswo engagiert*.

In order to account for the radicalism of Polanski's philosophical appropri-ation of Shakespeare's *Macbeth*, it is, as I suggested above, necessary to approach the film as both a psychobiographical and a sociocultural document. As far as Polanski's psychobiography is concerned, the relevant facts include both his past and his present, that is, the years between *Dance of the Vampires* and the *Macbeth* film. Roman Polanski was born in Paris in 1933, 'the year Hitler came to power' (*Roman* 4), but in 1936 his father, a Jewish Pole, unfor-tunately decided to return to his native country Poland and his native city Cracow. Hitler's forces invaded Poland in 1939, and the Polanski family 'had to wear white armbands with the Star [of David] on them in blue' (*Roman* 13). In 1941 Roman's mother, a Russian Jew, was sent to the concentration camp at Auschwitz, and soon after his father was caught in another roundup of Jews in Cracow. With both parents gone, Roman had to go into hiding with various families in or near Cracow. In 1945 Roman was reunited with his father, a survivor of Mathausen, an Austrian concentration camp. His mother did not survive Auschwitz.

In *Roman* Polanski describes his life as a Jewish boy inside the Cracow ghetto and on the run. There is not a trace of self-pity, but the traumatic impact of those formative years is clearly discernible, for instance, in the graphic recalling of an incident when the Polanski home was searched for illicit stocks of food (hoarding was forbidden in the ghetto). A tall German officer in peaked cap and glossy riding boots is inspecting the kitchen together with his mother, who has been persuaded by her husband to hide some rolls in a hatbox on top of a wardrobe:

> The officer returned, followed by my mother. We thought the inspection was over, but he lingered, smiling faintly, circling the room like a bird of prey, picking up my teddy-bear and swinging it by one leg, looking the place over. Suddenly, with the tip of his swagger stick, he reached up and flicked the hatbox off the top of the wardrobe. He picked it up, opened it, and scattered the rolls all over the floor. (*Roman* 17-18)

Thirty years later Polanski recreates or repeats (in the Freudian sense of the word) this very scene in his *Macbeth* film when the murderers dispatched by Macbeth burst in on Lady Macduff and her small son (IV.2.): 'I suddenly recalled how the SS officer had searched our room in the ghetto, swishing his riding crop to and fro, toying with my teddy bear, nonchalantly emptying out the hatbox full of forbidden bread' (*Roman* 291). Jewish childhood and boyhood in the Poland of the Nazi Holocaust, youth in the Poland of the Stalinist regime: Polanski would necessarily have to concur with Marek, one of his friends at the Lodz Film School in the fifties, when the latter made the following response to the question 'Is there a God or isn't there?' – a question put to him as 'an educated man' by Ziutek, a jovially 'plastered' policeman:

> 'Ziutek,' he said, 'if there is a God, he's a rotten old whore who watched what went on at Auschwitz and Hiroshima – who saw millions of innocent people murdered – and what kind of God is that? No, my friend, there isn't any God.' (*Roman* 106)

A decade or so later, when he was preparing the screenplay for *Rosemary's Baby* (1968), his first Hollywood movie, Polanski considered himself an agnostic who no more believed in Satan as evil incarnate than he believed in a personal God: 'the whole idea conflicted with my rational view of the world' (*Roman* 228). Consequently, he tried to make sure that Rosemary's supernatural experiences (the witches and warlocks, her impregnation by Satan himself, the fact that she eventually accepts responsibility for mothering the satanic baby, etc.) could be interpreted as 'figments of her imagination'

(*Roman* 228). *Rosemary's Baby*, which was both a critical and commercial success, turned him into 'something of a Hollywood golden boy' (*Roman* 245), and, soon after, this Hollywood golden boy married one of the Hollywood golden girls, the successful American actress Sharon Tate, in London. Indeed, golden time seemed, in Shakespeare's phrase, to have convented in Polanski's life:

> I was working with renewed relish. I had a wife I loved and a child on the way. I was still young enough to experience the strange, spine-tingling realization that happiness is here and now, not just around the corner or entombed in some golden memory of long ago. Professionally as well as personally, London in the early summer of 1969 was radiant with promise. (*Roman* 262)

Later that very same summer, on August 9, while Polanski was working on a new screenplay in London, Sharon Tate, more than eight months pregnant, was murdered in their Los Angeles home at Cielo Drive by four members of the so-called Manson family. She had been stabbed sixteen times, and, according to *Mass Murder: America's Growing Menace* (first published in 1985), her 'body lay in the living room of the house, a nylon rope tied tightly around her neck as though in preparation for a hanging'.[9] As far as the stabbing orgy is concerned, it is difficult to ignore the close resemblance between Sharon Tate's death and Polanski's choreography of Duncan's murder in the *Macbeth* film (Macbeth is seen to stab the king at least ten times). According to Thomas Kiernan's somewhat sensationalist reconstruction of the slaughter in *The Roman Polanski Story*, it was Susan Atkins (known in the Manson clan as Sadie Mae) who completed the gruesome stabbing of Sharon Tate, and who also had the obscene idea that 'she would cut the blond woman [Sharon Tate] open, take out the baby and bring it back to Charles Manson'.[10] However, there was not sufficient time for this caesarean operation, Susan Atkins later told a grand jury, but the traumatizing effect of the very idea might explain why Polanski, on two occasions in the film, has Macbeth visualize, in clinically gory detail, the 'bloody baby' Macduff being 'untimely ripp'd' from his mother's womb. Need I add, to complete this macabre study in Polanskian biography, that Sharon Tate's 'bloody baby' was also a boy?

Even though a perfectly ordinary, God-fearing couple, supermarket owner Leno LaBianca and his wife Rosemary [!], were killed in similar circumstances the following day, the attitude of Hollywood and the American media was clear from the start: Sharon Tate and her Polish husband had somehow brought this appalling tragedy on themselves 'by pursuing a kinky, dissolute, drug-oriented life style' (*Roman* 270). The press coverage of the slaughter at Cielo Drive provides a near-perfect endorsement of Jean Baudrillard's thesis that the Americans, with their 'postmodern' predilection for confusing art/simulacrum and life/reality, 'have no sense of simulation'.[11] Indeed, you may well wonder 'whether the [American] world itself isn't just here to serve as an advertising copy in some other world'.[12] Thus, according to *Time* (August 15), the Tate massacre represented 'a scene as grisly as anything depicted in Polanski's film explorations of the dark and melancholy corners of the human character' (*Roman* 271), while *Newsweek* (August 18), in a kind of *déjà lu*, states that 'the scene could hardly have been more bizarre had it appeared in one of Polish director Roman Polanski's own peculiarly nightmarish motion pictures'.[13] But *Newsweek* then goes on to describe the scene at Cielo Drive as if it *were* a film – 'Had there been cameras rolling as the door swung open, they would have captured the most chilling sight of all'[14] – and concludes with one more sickening twist to the film metaphor:

> In the end, she [Sharon Tate] took the lead role in a murder mystery far more tragic and macabre than Polanski could ever have crafted for her on the screen. 'Man,' gasped one detective, 'this is weirder than *Rosemary's Baby*.'[15]

Both Polanski himself (who was in London at the time of the murders) and his friend Jerzy Kosinsky were treated as official suspects by the Los Angeles police – the latter, a Polish *émigré* and trendily *outré* writer, simply because it seemed so natural to assume, in accordance with the Baudrillardean thesis, that he might well have lived out one of the more violent and perverse scenarios from his books. Besides, 'who knew', as a Los Angeles homicide detective candidly put it, 'what a bunch of Poles might be capable of doing'.[16] Polanski agreed to take a lie-detector test, which cleared him of any knowledge of or participation in the murders – at least as far as the police were concerned. The American press, however, still needed a villain and, in the absence of any hard facts, continued printing all kinds of bizarre rumours suggesting that the victims themselves were the true villains. Again it was argued – in accordance with the Baudrillardean thesis – that it was not at all surprising that real violence and terror should, in Thomas Kiernan's words, stalk and ultimately strike Polanski as 'a notoriously compulsive dealer in cinematic violence and terror': 'Had Polanski made nice, inoffensive films, went the conclusion, Sharon Tate and the others would still be alive. Somehow there was a direct causative connection between the murders and Polanski's moviemaking proclivities.'[17]

After four months of investigation the case broke, and the four Manson murderers were identified. There was, incidentally, no evidence that Charles Manson or his 'family' had ever seen a Polanski film or even knew who they had killed at Cielo Drive. But then, as the American composer John Moran proclaims in his Baudrillardean commentary to the CD version of his recent opera *The Manson Family* (1991), we are 'all aboard for a different truth', so 'which do you think is more real?'[18]

Polanski could now flee Los Angeles for Paris, the Swiss Alps, and London, where he contacted Kenneth Tynan, whom he had known since his early days in England, and proposed collaborating on a *Macbeth* screenplay. One effect of the Manson case had been a redoubling of Polanski's normal 'influx of ghoulish scripts', all of which he turned down, realizing that his next film would be scrutinized 'less for its quality than for its subject matter' (*Roman* 289). The Shakespearean subject matter of *Macbeth* would, he naively assumed, at least 'preserve [his] motives from suspicion' (*Roman* 297). In other words, Shakespeare the classic *par excellence* would be a reasonably safe bet under the circumstances. As Alfred Harbage notes in *Conceptions of Shakespeare*, the sociocultural phenomenon of Shakespeare idolatry, in which Polanski had decided to place his bet as an artistically serious film director, draws its strength from 'something other than its roots in the past': 'Having lost their anchorage in the faith of their fathers, many are seeking a substitute in secular literature, and perhaps, in a materialistic age, any form of idealism has something to be said for it.'[19]

Polanski's interest in Shakespeare can be traced back to his young days in Cracow. Inspired by Lawrence Olivier's *Hamlet* film, which he claims to have seen at least twenty times, he had 'read all of Shakespeare's plays in Polish and tried to imagine how they, too, would look as films' (*Roman* 49). Ever since he had wanted to make a film of one of Shakespeare's plays, and after Sharon Tate's death he felt that this 'might be the time' (*Roman* 289). The major tragedies, he thought, had already been admirably adapted for the screen, but *Macbeth* was the exception: 'Orson Welles [in *Macbeth* (1948)] and Kurosawa [in *Kumonusu-Djo/Throne of Blood* (1957)] had both tried with varying degrees of success – or, as I believed, of failure' (*Roman* 289). Generically as well as existentially, the choice of Shakespearean *tragedy* seems to have been a foregone conclusion, if we can trust his autobiography: the death of Sharon Tate had proved to be the only watershed in his life that really mattered. Before she died, he had 'sailed a boundless, untroubled sea of expectations and optimism':

> There used to be a tremendous fire within me – an unquenchable confidence that I could master anything if I really set my mind to it. This confidence was badly undermined by the killings and their aftermath. I not only developed a closer physical resemblance to my father after Sharon's death but began to take on some of his traits; his ingrained pessimism, his eternal dissatifaction with life, his profoundly Judaic sense of guilt, and his conviction that every joyous experience has its price. (*Roman* 283)

The *Macbeth* film can be seen as an almost Nietzschean articulation of Polanski's tragic *Weltanschauung* at this stage of his life, drawing, as it were, on both *The Will to Power* and *The Birth of Tragedy*. There is, first, the tragic sense of radical nihilism, which Nietzsche defined as 'the conviction of an absolute untenability of existence when it comes to the highest values one recognizes; plus the realization that we lack the least right to posit a beyond or an in-itself of things that might be "divine" or morality incarnate'.[20] Second, there is the tragic awareness of the barbaric or Dionysiac urges of the human mind, the witches' brew concocted of lust and cruelty: 'gerade die wildesten Bestien der Natur wurden [in the Dionysiac orgies of the Greek] entfesselt, bis zu jener abscheulichen Mischung von Wollust und Grausamkeit, die mir immer als der eigentliche "Hexentrank" erschienen ist'.[21] In the brilliant opening sequences of Polanski's film, this Dionysiac cauldron as well as the philosophical theme of radical nihilism, which have been *textually* fused into the witches' statement of 'Fair is foul, and foul is fair' (I.1.11), are expressed *cinematically* through a series of pregnant visual-spatial images.

The very first image, in the pre-credits sequence of the film, is a flat, arid landscape just before sunrise, perhaps a Martian desert with its steel-grey and blood-red tints, or a 'blank page of death' like Paul Auster's Great Salt Desert in *Moon Palace*[22] – a cosmic wasteland of total silence, 'without form, and void', as the Book of Genesis describes pre-creation earth. As the murky light of a misty, clouded Scottish November day breaks through, we realize that we find ourselves on some sand flats in that grey tidal area between ebb and flow, land and sea, which is neither landscape nor seascape, but an unnatural void, 'a breach in nature', to quote Macbeth's words about Duncan's 'gash'd stabs' (II.3.111). It is on this cosmic *tabula rasa* that the three Weird Sisters, two old witches and one young, now proceed to inscribe their evil code, that is, the *Macbeth* scenario. The horizontal line of the sand flats is broken, cut through, not by a vertical line, but by a crooked, diagonal line, viz. the stick belonging to the oldest and ugliest witch. This crooked stick now draws a circle, from which the sand is scooped up, and in the hole are buried, first a noose, then a severed hand with a dagger – the fatal dagger to be deployed later in the murder of King Duncan. Finally, the Weird Sisters seal their evil inscription on the cosmic slate by emptying a phial of blood onto the sand. They agree to meet again on the heath, after the hurly-burly of some battle, to deal with Macbeth himself, and we watch them walk away and vanish in the fog and filthy air.

This opening scene is followed by the credits, accompanied, on the sound track, by the hurly-burly of the battle prophesied by the witches. Immediately after the credits we are returned to the sand flats of the pre-credits sequence, and we now appreciate the symbolic significance of the red Martian vista at the start: the sand flats have become the site of a battleground littered with dead or dying soldiers. Indeed, the very first human action we witness on the screen is that of a soldier brutally finishing off another soldier by bashing in his back so that blood seeps through his tunic. Mars is the god of war, and red the colour of blood, or, to quote John Arden on the traditional colour symbolism that he utilized in his play *Serjeant Musgrave's Dance*: 'Red is for murder, and for the soldier's coat.'[23]

More blood fills the screen when the 'bloody man' (I.2.1), a soldier bleeding profusely from his wounds, reports from the recent battle against rebels and invading armies how brave Macbeth faced the merciless Macdonwald 'with

46

bloody execution', 'unseam'd him from the nave to th'chops,/ And fix'd his head upon our battlements' (I.2.18, 22-3). Shakespeare's *Macbeth* is 'bloody business' throughout (blood is mentioned over a hundred times in the play), so Jan Kott is surely right to point out that 'a production of *Macbeth* not evoking a picture of the world flooded with blood would inevitably be false'. And a play like *Titus Andronicus* offers ample proof that Shakespeare himself was not exactly averse to the cruder 'splatter' or 'slasher' effects of what is generically known as the Elizabethan revenge tragedy. Shakespeare bardolaters have traditionally questioned the bard's sole authorship (the sheer brutality of both the rape and the revenge were deemed unworthy of Shakespeare), but, as Sylvan Barnet regretfully has to conclude in his introduction to the Signet edition of *Titus Andronicus* (1963), 'however displeased we may be by part or all of *Titus*, there is no evidence that it is not his'.[24]

The American reception of Polanski's *Macbeth* film testifies to the supremacy of a corresponding quasi-religious bardolatry amongst film reviewers. Originally, a spectacular Royal Command Performance had been scheduled for December 1971 in London, but, to Polanski's dismay and disappointment, Columbia Pictures cancelled this London opening in favour of a New York premiere in January at Hugh Hefner's newly acquired Playboy Theatre on West 57th Street (after all, it was Hefner's Playboy Enterprises that had put up the money for the film). Most American reviewers were acutely displeased by what they regarded as Polanski's sacrilegious treatment of Shakespeare's classic play and expressed horror at the gory violence and twisted morbidity of the film, which they deemed entirely unworthy of the bard. Reviewing the film for the Chicago *Sun-Times*, Roger Ebert found Polanski's characters (*not* Shakespeare's, even though they appear to be acting and speaking in accord with the bard's authentic text most of the time) 'anti-intellectual, witless and driven by deep, shameful wells of lust and violence'.[25] For *Women's Wear Daily* critic Gail Rock, the film is 'an assault on the audience that seems [to her] to divert us from the intellectual thrust of *Macbeth* and turn us into voyeurs of a killing spree that makes Manson and his friends pale in comparison'.[26] So Charles Manson strikes back from his prison cell – and he does it again and again, in review after review. Quite a few American reviewers appear to be lost in what might be called a Baudrillardean Bermuda Triangle, that is, a kind of an epistemological/hermeneutical *Horizontverschmelzung*, in which the trinity of Polanski, Manson, and Macbeth is fashioned into a variety of rich and strange configurations. In *Newsweek* Paul D. Zimmerman found that 'parallels between the Manson murders (which took Polanski's wife Sharon Tate) and the mad, bloody acts of these beautiful, lost Macbeths keep pressing themselves on the viewer – as though Shakespeare's play has provided Polanski with some strange opportunity to act out his own complicated feelings about Satanism, mystic ties, blood, evil and revenge'.[27] And Zimmerman concludes his review with the following rhetorical question and answer:

'Is the decapitation of Macbeth and the parading of his head on a spear an indispensable reality? If so, then *Macbeth* is a work of art – in the grand manner of Buchenwald, Lidice and, yes, the Manson murders.'[28]

So Zimmerman seems to have gone one better here, adding Hitler to the satanic Polanski-Manson-Macbeth trinity. In terms of this quadrangular configuration, Polanski is not only equated with Manson and Macbeth, he is also – never mind his personal experience, as a Polish-Jewish victim, of the Nazi Holocaust – identified with Hitler. As a rule, however, critics stick to the well-worn parallels with the Manson murders, asking questions like 'How do we account for this man who apparently has decided to make us pay for the tragic murder of his wife and friends by demonically bathing us in vomitous film horror?'[29] Pauline Kael's review in *The New Yorker* is exceptional in so far as she explicitly – albeit with 'an element of guilt and embarrassment' – endorses the Baudrillardean thesis in her argument. There was, she argues, 'an eery element' that she and the American public responded to: 'Even though we knew that Roman Polanski had nothing whatever to do with causing the murder of his wife and unborn child and friends, the massacre seemed a vision realised from his nightmare movies.'[30] Regrettably, Kael notes, Polanski himself 'didn't quite understand that this connection was inevitable'. With a proper understanding of postmodern American mentality, he would not have complained about those who reviewed his films in terms of the Manson murders (in an interview in *The New York Times* Polanski had complained that whereas 'what happened [in the Manson case] was reviewed in terms of my films', it was now 'vice versa': 'Now my films are reviewed in terms of what happened [in the Manson case].'[31] Kael detects, in Polanski's position, 'either a strange form of naïveté or a divided consciousness' [!], and, having evidently rid herself of the last element of guilt and embarrassment, she concludes: 'One sees the Manson murders in this *Macbeth* because the director has put them there.'[32] For the record: Polanski did not put the 'bloody business', the gory violence, in *Macbeth*, for it was already there, in Shakespeare's play, to 'inform' the director's eyes, his unique cinematic vision, which was of course coloured (that goes without saying) by his equally unique experiential background, his direct exposure to modern history from Hitler to Manson.

Shakespeare's *Macbeth* is a violent play, and Polanski 'never believed in cop-outs', in life or in art. 'You have to show violence the way it is,' he told a reporter for the *New York Times* when the film was released. 'If you don't show it realistically, that's immoral and harmful.'[33] Still, as Polanski correctly observes in his autobiography, the *Macbeth* film contains 'only a fraction of the gore that characterizes any Peckinpah movie' (*Roman* 297). There is nothing comparable, say, with the terrifying gun battles – orgies of killing, optically reinforced by a sophisticated real-time/slow-motion montage – in Peckinpah's landmark Western *The Wild Bunch* (1969). What is comparable, however, is Peckinpah's line of response to the question why he had not made a film about the Vietnam War, if he wanted to deal realistically with contemporary American violence – apart from the genocidal war in Vietnam (epitomized by the My Lai massacre), this was also the decade of political assassinations in the US). 'The Western,' he explained, 'is a universal frame within which it is possible to comment on today.'[34] Polanski had also assumed that Shakespeare's classic *Macbeth* could serve as a kind of universal frame, within which his motives might be preserved from suspicion.

In London the film was launched at a gala opening on February 2 at the Plaza Theatre in Piccadilly Circus, and the acclaim *Macbeth* received from the British film critics contrasts significantly with the earlier American reception. Frivolous British headlines such as 'Macbrilliant' and 'Macbeth Is A Winner' conceal, as Polanski rightly notes, 'a far more literate and adventurous perception of filmed Shakespeare' (*Roman* 297-98). Apart from a sturdy British common sense precluding any Baudrillardean (con)fusions of art and reality, the more congenial reception of Polanski's film in Britain (and Europe) must, I think, also be ascribed to a cultural literacy that was, by comparison, more at home in such phenomena as the Theatre of the Absurd, of Cruelty – and of Nudity. Thus American prudery-cum-bardolatry had connected Lady Macbeth's nudity in the sleepwalking scene to the Playboy financing. As the critic in the *New York Daily Mirror* so fastidiously phrased it: 'Francesca Annis [the twenty-five-year-old actress that played the part of Lady Macbeth] comes across like a spot-crazy Playboy bunny' (*Roman* 297). No such prudish sniggering in swinging London where Kenneth Tynan, Polanski's collaborator on the *Macbeth* screenplay, had recently staged his notorious erotic revue *Oh! Calcutta!*. According to Helen Dawson's assessment in *Plays and Players* (September 1970), this revue had crashed the nudity barrier once and for all by virtue of its 'bold and triumphant attack on the taboos which have hedged in the Western theatre for centuries'.

Polanski's close affiliations with the Theatre of the Absurd, the existential philosophies of absurdism or nihilism, radical nihilism à la Nietzsche, have already been touched upon in my discussion of the appropriation of Shakespeare's *Macbeth*. In *The Theatre of the Absurd* (first published in 1961), Martin Esslin also stresses the Nietzschean heritage by quoting the famous lines in *Also Sprach Zarathustra*: 'Can it be possible! This old saint in the forest has not yet heard that God is dead!'[35] Underlying the 'absurdity' of major playwrights like Samuel Becket, Arthur Adamov, Eugène Ionesco, and Harold Pinter is the philosophical awareness, Esslin argues, that 'the decline of religious belief has deprived man of certainties', and that 'it is no longer possible to accept complete closed systems of values and revelations of divine purpose'.[36] It is not surprising then, given the absurdist climate of European arts and literature in those days, that the general reception of Polanski's *Macbeth* film here would be more positive and congenial than in America. Thus one might, for instance, expect a more tolerant or even appreciative response to Polanski's absurdist interpretation/appropriation of *Macbeth*, the fact that the absurdism of Macbeth's sound-and-fury monologue after his wife's suicide (V.5.16-28) has been extended, as it were, to the whole play, including the ending. It is surely no coincidence that Tom Stoppard's breakthrough as a successful playwright in modern British theatre a few years earlier was also founded on an absurdist interpretation/appropriation of Shakespeare with *Rosencrantz and Guildenstern Are Dead* (1967).

Even though Polanski insists on showing violence the way it is, that is, realistically (because otherwise it would be 'immoral and harmful'), there are few gratuitous, sensationalist 'aggro-effects' in the *Macbeth* film: most of the violence shown is the normal violence of a feudal regime founded on professional soldiery. 'Aggro-effects' is the term coined by Edward Bond for the deliberate shock or alienation effects that he employs in his special version of the Theatre of Cruelty, for instance, in the notorious baby-stoning sequence in *Saved* (1966) and in the torture scene in *Lear* (1972) where the straitjacketed King Lear's eyes are gouged out by a device 'perfected on dogs for removing human eyes'.[37] Apropos of the latter play, Bond's version of Shakespeare's *King Lear*, it is worth noting that by far the most radical appropriations and modernizations of Shakespeare have happened in the theatre and not on the screen: both Stoppard and Bond have *rewritten* their Shakespeare, from a modernist/absurdist and an anarchist/primitivist perspective, respectively. But several years before Bond's 'aggro-effective' *Lear*, the Royal Shakespeare Company had developed its own Theatre of Cruelty, 'a habit', to quote Laurence Kitchin's *Drama in the Sixties*, 'of lingering over the cruelty, of spelling it out'.[38] Thus Gloucester's ill-treatment by the servants in a production of *King Lear*, for instance, was 'an extra, an inspiration of the director, Peter Brook'.[39] For as a Shakespeare director Brook had long been fascinated and inspired by the French director, actor and writer Antonin Artaud and his manifestos, *Theatre of Cruelty 1 and 2*. Artaud had argued that the true *raison d'être* of modern theatre was, through some kind of shock tactics, to remind mankind of the inexorable non-human forces that control its life and destiny. Let me cite a few passages from his *Theatre and the Plague* by way of illustration:

> All great myths are dark.... One cannot imagine all the great Fables aside from a mood of danger, torture, and bloodshed, telling the masses about the original division of the sexes and the slaughter that came with creation.... The theatre will never find itself again ... except by furnishing the spectator with the truthful precipitates of dreams, in which his taste for crime, his erotic obsessions, his savagery, his chimeras, his utopian sense of life and matter, even his cannibalism, pour out on a level not counterfeit and illusory, but interior.[40]

The most Artaudesque effect in the *Macbeth* film is, I think, the shock of physical nakedness that the audience experiences when Macbeth visits the witches' coven (the idea of the coven, incidentally, derives from Polanski's preceding cinematic exercise in the demonic, *Rosemary's Baby*). The dark non-human or sub-human power that controls Macbeth's destiny is here epitomized by the shocking nudity of the ugly hags around the steaming cauldron. Only a few of the violent and bloody images in the film can be described as truly Artaudesque, but, as such exceptions to the Polanskian rule of cinematic realism or naturalism, one could perhaps single out the hanging of the Thane of Cawdor, the stabbing of King Duncan, and, of course, the lopping off of Macbeth's head at the end.

Polanski's Macbeth film is embedded in the complex and confused cultural practice of modern Shakespeare reception and appropriation. Paradoxically, this cultural practice, by its obsessive need to modernize, reread and rewrite Shakespeare in order to make him 'our contemporary', refutes the very claim which is its ideological foundation, viz. that Shakespeare was, in Ben Jonson's words, 'not of an age, but for all time', transcending, by virtue of his genius, time and place as the bearer of universal truth. As John Drakakis concludes in his introduction to *Alternative Shakespeares*:

> In concrete historical terms Shakespeare can never be 'our contemporary' except by the strategy of appropriation, yet [*sic*] the protean values which which subsequent generations of critics have discovered in the texts themselves can be demonstrated to be in large part the projections of their own externally applied values.[41]

The name of this Shakespeare game – as distinct from, say, the academic game of Shakespearean scholarship – is *modern appropriation*, and in my case study I have tried to identify the 'externally applied values' that Polanski chose to project into *his* Shakespeare text, the *Macbeth* film. These values – existential as well as cultural – are, as I have shown, functions of the specific times and places in which Polanski lived and worked. However, as a cinematic work of modern Shakespeare appropriation the film is only a limited success, at least if measured against the artistic standards of Polanski films like *Rosemary's Baby*, *Chinatown* (1974), and *Tess* (1979). The problem lies, I suggest, in the crucial process of appropriation, and it is a philosophical as well as an artistic problem. What it boils down to is simply that the supernaturalism of Shakespeare's Weird Sisters proves to be too weird for Polanski's cinematic universe, which is basically a naturalistic universe, philosophically as well as artistically. In *Rosemary's Baby* Polanski could negotiate the supernaturalism by ensuring that the weird happenings could also be interpreted as figments of Rosemary's sick imagination. But in the *Macbeth* film there is no negotiation whatsoever, probably due to a bardolatrous respect for the sanctity of Shakespeare's text, so the supernaturalism is taken on board, lock, stock and barrel, and the result is an increasing overload of refractory ideas and images for which Polanski's cinematic imagination fails to find adequate – to apply T.S. Eliot's well-worn critical concept – objective correlatives (witness the surprisingly inept realization of the Birnam-wood-coming-to-Dunsinane sequence). As a Polanski film, *Macbeth* is an interesting failure (in my jaundiced view, the great majority of Shakespeare films would have to be written off as devoid of artistic interest, so I am far from damning with faint praise). The reason why *Macbeth* fails as a film, then, is that Polanski's appropriation is incomplete or half-hearted, leaving, for instance, an artistically unbridgeable gap between Shakespeare's supernaturalism and the modern director's naturalism. Had the process of appropriation been allowed to run its full course (as it was in Polanski's adaptation of Thomas Hardy's *Tess of the d'Urbervilles*), Shakespeare's text might have suffered, in the bard's own beautiful phrase, a sea change into something rich and strange, that is, an authentic Polanski movie.

Notes

1. William Shakespeare, *Macbeth*, ed. Kenneth Muir (London: Methuen, 1976); further references are also to this edition.
2. Peter Brook, Preface to Jan Kott's *Shakespeare Our Contemporary* (London: Methuen, 1965), pp. x-xi.
3. Jan Kott, *Shakespeare Our Contemporary* (London: Methuen, 1965), p. 90.
4. Roman Polanski, *Roman* (London: Heinemann, 1984), p. 297. Polanski's autobiography is hereafter cited in the text as *Roman* followed by page reference.
5. Kenneth Tynan, *A View of the English Stage* (Frogmore, St Albans, Herts: Paladin, 1976), p. 12.
6. Tynan, p. 12.
7. E. Pearlman, '"Macbeth" on Film: Politics', *Shakespeare Survey*, No. 39, p. 71.
8. Paul Werner, *Roman Polanski* (Frankfurt am Main: Fischer, 1981), pp. 136-7.
9. Jack Levin and James Alan Fox, *Mass Murder: America's Growing Menace* (New York: Berkley, 1991), pp. 78-9.
10. Thomas Kiernan, *The Roman Polanski Story* (New York: Delilah/Grove Press, 1980), p. 224.
11. Jean Baudrillard, *America* (London and New York: Verso, 1989), p. 28.
12. Baudrillard, p. 32.
13. Barabara Leaming, *Polanski: His Life and Films* (London: Hamish Hamilton, 1982), p. 71.
14. Leaming, p. 71.
15. Leaming, pp. 71-2.
16. Kiernan, p. 235.
17. Kiernan, p. 238.
18. John Moran, *The Manson Family: An Opera* (Germany: Point Music/A joint venture of Euphorbia Productions Ltd and Philips Classics Productions, 1992), I.iii.
19. Alfred Harbage, *Conceptions of Shakespeare* (Cambridge, Mass.: Harvard University Press, 1966), p. 38.
20. Friedrich Nietzsche, *The Will to Power*, ed. W. Kaufmann (New York: Random House, 1968), p. 9.

21. Friedrich Nietzsche, *Die Geburt der Tragödie*, in: G. Colli and M. Montinari (eds), *Friedrich Nietzsche: Sämtliche Werke*, Band I (München: Verlag de Gruyter, 1980), p. 32.
22. Paul Auster, *Moon Palace* (London: Faber and Faber, 1989), p. 154.
23. John Arden, 'Telling a True Tale', in: C. Marowitz, T. Milne and O. Hale (eds), *The Encore Reader* (London: Methuen, 1970), p. 127.
24. Quoted by Eugene M. Waith in his introduction to *Titus Andronicus* (Oxford: Oxford University Press, 1984), p. 13.
25. Quoted by Leaming, p. 87.
26. Leaming, p. 87.
27. Leaming, pp. 86-7.
28. Leaming, p. 88.
29. Quoted by Kiernan, p. 240.
30. Quoted by Leaming, p. 87.
31. Leaming, p. 86.
32. Leaming, p. 87.
33. Quoted by Kiernan, p. 241.
34. Quoted by John Wakeman (ed.), *World Film Directors*, Vol. II: 1945-1985 (New York: H.W. Wilson, 1988), p. 759.
35. Martin Esslin, *The Theatre of the Absurd* (Harmondsworth, Middlesex: Penguin, 1970), p. 389.
36. Esslin, p. 391.
37. Edward Bond, *Lear* (London: Eyre Methuen, 1986), p. 63.
38. Laurence Kitchin, *Drama in the Sixties: Form and Interpretation* (London: Faber and Faber, 1966), p. 22.
39. Kitchin, p. 22.
40. Quoted by John Elsom, *Post-war British Theatre* (London, Henley and Boston: Routledge & Kegan Paul, 1976), p. 144.
41. John Drakakis (ed.), *Alternative Shakespeares* (London and New York: Methuen, 1985), p. 24.

Peter Brook's *King Lear*: A Reassessment

Michael Mullin

The appearance in 1971 of Peter Brook's filmed *King Lear* marks the end-point, so far as theatre history is concerned, of an evolution that began in rehearsals for the 1962 stage production in Stratford-upon-Avon. The complex interrelationships between Brook's stage and film versions of the play account in large measure for the extraordinary position of his controversial film as a major production of *King Lear* at mid-century. Whether acclaimed or decried, Brook's interpretation cannot be ignored, for it raises the fundamental questions: What is *King Lear*? The various texts? Fully realized stage productions? Or textually altered films such as Brook's *Lear* or, more extreme, Kurosawa's *Ran*?

In 1962, when Brook began to rehearse *King Lear*, he had already made his mark at Stratford-upon-Avon in 1955 as the innovative director of *Titus Andronicus* starring Laurence Olivier and Vivien Leigh. In 1960 he had joined the newly christened Royal Shakespeare Company at Stratford as director of experimental projects; his production of *Lear* was to be the first full-scale experiment.[1] Scofield, who had worked with Brook before, came to *Lear* fresh from his success as Sir Thomas More in *A Man For All Seasons*. When *King Lear* finally opened on 6 November 1962, having been delayed for two months by Scofield's poor health, it immediately provoked controversy. Looking for an antidote to the 1959 *Lear*, sentimentalized by Charles Laughton in the title role, audiences encountered a new *Lear*, unsoftened by sentimentality or spectacle, superbly acted throughout yet austere and bereft of redemption.[2] The stage was bare, without scenery and with only a rough wooden throne, a bench, or a table, carried on as needed and as quickly cleared. Upstage two giant white screens rose up in front of the cyclorama to form an abstract backdrop. This setting remained unchanged except for the storm scene. Then, as the storm sounds grew louder, three huge rust-colored iron thundersheets descended from the flies above, trembling as they made the thunder. Lit by a harsh white light, Lear spoke as the others onstage mimed the storm's effects, his speeches and their replies punctuated by the crash of thunder and the wailing of the wind.[3] Costumes were of leather, thick, worn, and ill-fitting, in various shades of black and brown, with only a hint of color here and there – the Fool's red hat, or the crimson lining of Lear's cloak.

At the center of this critically acclaimed production, widely thought to have been influenced by Samuel Beckett and Jan Kott,[4] was Paul Scofield's King Lear. His head close-cropped, his voice at first harsh and growling, then growing soft and sometimes breaking, Scofield established Lear as a strong virile tyrant, whose word was law and who commanded both fear and respect. Philip Hope-Wallace (*Manchester Guardian*, 13 December 1963), for instance, described him as 'an old sea dog' in whom 'the pathos of old age [is] utterly convincing, terrible and touching, without a hint of sentimentality or the effect of enjoying his griefs'. Yet not every critic agreed that his was all to the good. In fact, many complained that Lear's grandeur had been lost and that the music had gone from the poetry. Speaking for many academic critics, Maynard Mack believed that by 'rationalizing' Lear's behaviour and giving sympathetic support to Goneril and Regan's displeasure, Brook and Scofield had diminished the play's pathos, if not its horror.[5]

The film that emerged from this enormously successful production had a strange beginning. As we learn from Roger Manvell, Brook and the producer, Michael Birkett, literally took the play apart and re-assembled it.[6] At one point they brought in the poet Ted Hughes to 'translate' the text. Then realizing that this would not work, Brook wrote his own prose narrative without dialogue. Even the shooting script underwent several revisions.[7] As a result, the film departs so drastically from Shakespeare's text that, however appreciative of Brook's artistry, most critics have treated the film as an adaptation rather than a realization of the play.[8] In cutting a four-hour plus play text to make a two-hour film, it is not surprising that great swathes of Shakespeare disappeared. Nor is it surprising that the director, whose credits included *Marat/Sade* (1964) and the Vietnam protest play *US* (1966), chose to slice out anything that smelled of kindness, humor, or humanity.[9] What is unusual is what remains of the earlier stage production, once one has allowed for the sea change in moving from stage to screen.

That change is great, and it deserves examination. In an interview in 1966, Brook had doubted that a Shakespeare film was even possible, arguing that the film's insistent localization was unable to match the mobility of thought and place offered by the non-localized space of the theatre:

> The film creates a plausible world in which the action can reasonably unfold, but the price we pay for this plausible world are the complexities that cannot be encompassed and demonstrated. That is, the problem of filming Shakespeare is one of finding ways of shifting gears, styles, and conventions as lightly and deftly on the screen as within the mental processes reflected by Elizabethan blank verse onto the screen of the mind.[10]

Although he tried to compensate by an unconventional film style, when Brook moved *Lear* from the stage to the screen, major changes were inevitable.

Moving *King Lear* from the abstract environment of the bare stage to the rugged winter countryside of Jutland forced Brook to specify the location of the play's action, and this in turn affected its narrative structure. Although broken up by discontinuities and bizarre camerawork, with its three 'castles' and the seashore at the end, the terrain gives a fundamental unity to the action. The narrative unfolds as a series of journeys across this terrain, with a major episode at each resting place. The film opens in Lear's 'castle', in the throne room, and then it moves outside. We see Kent riding away, and then on the road we see two crude horse-drawn wagons covered with furs and accompanied by mounted escorts. The two groups separate. Interior shots of the wagons reveal that one holds Goneril and Regan; the other, Gloucester, Edmund, and Edgar.

The action then moves to 'Goneril's Castle', announced by a title with additional explanation: 'The banished Duke of Kent is now disguised as a servant. He seeks employment with the King, who is now living with his daughter Goneril.' The castle's interior spaces are established as a private room with a fire (where Goneril and Albany talk over dinner) and a large hall where Lear and his rowdy knights feed. Outside is a courtyard into which Lear retreats after cursing Goneril. From it, Lear's wagon and horsemen rumble forth, heading for Regan's castle. The scene shifts, as we learn from another title, to 'Gloucester's castle. Where Edmund, bastard son of the Duke of Gloucester, plots against his brother Edgar'. And the action moves inside the castle for a scene (snippets from I.1 and II.1, 2 and 3) showing Edmund's hoodwinking of Gloucester, Edgar's escape, and Edmund's cover-up. Once more the location changes. Lear arrives at Regan's castle, only to learn that she has left. Another title brings us back to Gloucester's castle, where Kent is stocked in the frigid courtyard and where Lear and his train enter. After Lear confronts Regan, Goneril's wagon and her entourage roll into the yard, and at the end of the episode, shouting and roaring, Lear drives out into the storm lashing his frenzied horses. The scenes that follow locate the heath where Lear and his company wander somewhere outside the castle walls, in contrast to the warm room inside the castle where the others remain. After the mock trial in a hovel attached to the castle, Lear is lifted into a wagon, sending him on his way to Dover. Goneril and Edmund leave in their wagon to prepare for war, and, after Gloucester's blinding, the action moves to the battlefields near the seashore, thereafter switching from one indeterminate place to another to end on the beach.

Faced with the need to make sense of the specific landscape and dwellings the film portrays, Brook made the journeys from castle to castle an important part of the narrative, not only so that its concern becomes what happens in a given place, but how people get themselves from one place to another. In the process the director had to restructure the narrative, rearranging large parts of the text, and bringing together words and actions which Shakespeare kept dispersed, greatly simplifying the contrapuntal movement between plot and subplots.

With the film's shooting script providing this episodic framework, the dialogue was placed within it. Reversing the normal process of theatrical production, where actors seek to discover how to realize the words of the script, Brook seems to have worked backwards (or inside out), from a visualization of the film as a series of distinct episodes linked by journeys to selection of dialogue, skipping from one scene to another. Like the 'collage Shakespeare' taken up by Brooks's assistant Charles Marowitz during the mid-1960s and early 1970s, the *Lear* filmscript – the actual text of the play as spoken on the soundtrack – defies compact description.

In somewhat the same way as Brook used Shakespeare's text as the initial inspiration and then returned to it for dialogue after restructuring the play in cinematic terms, he used his theatre production as a reservoir of ideas. In the film he sought effects similar to those he achieved in the theatre. Some are general and obvious. In the theatre, many of the effects and much of the acting were stylized, the storm scenes especially. Down from the flies came three huge iron thundersheets, powdery with rust, which trembled and sounded the thunder that punctuated Lear's speeches. There was the sound of wind, but no lightning flashed. Rather, the stage was fully lit, and the actors mimed the effects of the storm in a ballet-like sequence. In the film, Brook uses another kind of stylization – jump cuts, dissolves, visual discontinuity, fades to black, superposed images – to create the efect of the storm on Lear's mind.[11] Here the transference from theatre to film simply doesn't work – just as some the stylization in the theatre didn't work either.

More difficult to judge is the carry-over from theatre to film of the actors' interpretations. Imbedded in the film are performances by Scofield, Irene Worth, and Alan Webb in the roles they played first onstage; the Lear, the Goneril, and the Gloucester we see in the film square with the characterizations described by the theatre critics. Even with a different set, a different supporting cast, a different script, and a different medium, the sense of character behind the acting of these principals seems whole and consistent. It is this strong link between the film and the theatre production that is most difficult to trace and describe. For it is not a matter of whether Scofield said a line one way in the theatre and another way on film – he undoubtedly varied his performance over the three years in production in any case – but rather that, viewing the film, one can get a sense of the character he portrayed in the theatre. So, too, with Irene Worth and Alan Webb, the film offers a glimpse not of what the actors looked like onstage but of the characters the audience responded to. In this very special sense, the film is a window through which we can look to see performances otherwise lost with the closing of the production.

Turning from these strong conceptual links – the surreal 'Brechtian' style and the actors' interpretations of the central characters – one can discern other points of contact between the stage and the film productions. Consider the stage business. To begin the play, in the theatre Brook used some stage business to establish the occasion and then invented a ceremony for Lear's division of his kingdom. On the bare stage, downstage right stands a crude throne; near it, upstage center, a rough-hewn table; facing it, stage left, benches. To the table comes Kent, attended by a servant who puts a medal and chain of office around his neck. Then in come the others, who talk as they straighten their cloaks and put on gloves in preparation for the King's entrance. Lear enters, and the ceremony begins. He sits on the throne and signals to Kent, who goes to Goneril. She rises from the bench and takes 'the orb' of state from him. Then she goes to the King holding the orb in outstretched hands while reciting her protestation of devotion. She lowers the orb, curtseys, and returns to her seat on the bench. At a signal from Lear, Kent unrolls the map, and the King marks her portion on it. Regan follows suit, taking the orb, speaking, curtseying, and sitting to hear her patrimony proclaimed. Cordelia, who sits furthest downstage, confides her fears directly to the audience. She fails the test, and when Kent rebukes the King, Lear rises and seizes a sword, rushes at Kent, and then flings the sword away, shouting 'Hear me, recreant!' (I.1. 168). In the film, the occasion is established by a long pan across a crowd of the King's subjects, their faces frozen in wide-mouthed fear, in the courtyard; then the scene shifts to the council chamber, and the ceremony begins with a close-up of Lear's face, eyes hooded, alert, taking in everyone in the room as he utters the fateful words: 'Know that we have divided in three our kingdom' (I.1. 36-37). Truncated, the ceremony of the orbs remains, but the medieval fortress, which now replaces the open stage, and Brook's relentless nihilism combine to simplify the scene's complexity, keeping Cordelia silent, eliminating the banter that opens the play, and giving full scope to the brooding, volcanic energies that Scofield's Lear seems just barely able to control.[12] In this scene the stage business of the orb remains in film only as an artifact, a useful bit that they decided to keep.

A different kind of transference from stage to screen occurs, during what the promptbook calls the 'Hunting Scene' (I.4). In a bold piece of stage business that surprised audiences, Scofield as Lear entered from hunting with his whip in his hand, soon followed by his rowdy knights, who shouted for dinner. Throughout the scene, they remained, a rough and ready onstage audience for the King. Their jeers and taunts encouraged the King when he confronted Oswald, and they helped Kent corner and then pummel him. The climax came when, exploding at Goneril's quite accurate description of his roughnecks, Lear shouted 'Darkness and devils!' and, the promptbook says, there were 'tables thrown over, noise, confusion'. 'As Lear overturned the table, the stage exploded and sent shrapnel flying in a dozen different directions,' wrote Charles Marowitz, recalling the scene in rehearsal.[13] It was, Marowitz said, 'the one moment in the production which is dangerously unpredictable'. In the film, the riotous hundred who could only be suggested by ten actors onstage grew to something convincingly near that number. The simple tables carried onto the bare stage at the beginning of the scene became a fully realized medieval banqueting hall with a roaring fireplace, a kind of balcony along one side (from which Goneril and Albany can be seen looking down with disgust and some alarm at the crew below), and a great solid door through which Lear rushed, followed by his men, at the end of the scene. In one sense, the film's insistent physicality and specificity reduce the scene's symbolic power, making it merely an exciting medieval tumult – a re-make of the bar-room brawls of the Westerns.

Yet, in another sense, it remains true to the idea of the stage production, stripping Lear of any claims to sympathy and demonstrating how extreme his behavior has become. In this sense, and it is surely quite fundamental, the scene on film realizes the essentials of the stage production. As for the film as a whole, only in these two instances – the ceremony of the orbs and the riot at Goneril's – is there a direct transfer from the staging and stage business to the film. True, there are moments, such as Gloucester's blinding and his fall, to name just two, when the film and the stage production coincide, depicting similar actions. Yet these actions are common to any performance of the play, and even here the staging differs significantly from the film. In the blinding scene onstage, Cornwall signals the servants to tip back the chair holding Gloucester so that he can use his spur to put out his eye. In the film, Cornwall reaches around to the table behind him to get a spoon, one of the props that help make the setting medieval, and uses its curved handle to gouge out the eye. So, too, thinking he falls from Dover cliffs, onstage Gloucester rolls and tumbles from center stage down to the forestage. In the film he and Edgar are seen in extreme close-up speaking together just before the fall, and the effect of falling then comes from the camerawork, the camera pulling back to reveal the two small figures alone on the beach. In text, in setting, in acting, and in all but a few details of staging or stage business, the stage production and the film differ greatly.

Despite these differences, the film and the stage production share a vision of the play that is essentially the same. As with any performance of any play, it is reductive, choosing from the text's many possibilities those which can be realized by a particular group of actors working together with a particlar director at a particular time in history. Brook recognized this limitation. In fact, he took it as a given. 'A performance,' he said recently, is a crucible in which influences are playing and producing different influences, different results. So that the production I did of Lear was a production of Shakespeare's play as a group of actors and myself, together, could best understand that play at the moment.... Now a play that's been written in the past meets the present; but a play can't meet the present because 'a play' is a generalization and 'the present' is a generalization. It only meets the present through specific circumstances ... a band of people at a given place and at a given time.[14]

When Charles Marowitz was observing the shaping of this *Lear* in rehearsal, he witnessed the beginning of a process that reached its final, fixed form in Brook's film. In the theatre it is asumed that many of the interpretations that inform the actors' and the director's voices will never get past the footlights. Of these interprtations, each a practical reading of the play tested in the laboratory of actual performance, we learn only indirectly – an interview in the press, rehearsal notes, theatre talk. The performance itself is open-ended, leaving to the audience a wide range of responses as it enters into the creation. In Brook's stage production, more was suggested than was depicted or represented. The abstract settings ensured that the acting would come near stylization, even when it was most naturalistic – how can anyone act naturally on a weird, surreal set without being fundamentally un-natural? The same aesthetic holds for the film, yet with important differences. The director's intentions are boldly, even garishly manifest. Given the discontinuities in the script and the action, the characters' personalities are sharply etched; although, with so much of the text unspoken, their complex thoughts and feelings remain inarticulate. And, finally, perhaps most important, the film is permanent. It lasts, while the theatre production, now recorded only in the promptbooks and a sheaf of photographs and reviews, has vanished with its last performance.

Viewed as the end point in a collaboration among artists who lived with the play and tried to interpret it during the 1960s, Brook's *Lear* on film is an important document in the play's critical history. By no means a 'performance' of the play, the film gives us a raw, sometimes hysterical demonstration of what the 'subtext' (to use a 1960s buzzword) had come to mean to Brook. Brook's outrage at the war in Vietnam and his own alienation from establishment culture screams out through the film. No sentimentality! No humor! No redemption! As the film recedes in time, its value as a reading of the play will become clearer. As it is, it is a valuable document in the play's history because it brings us close to Brook's vision and to the acting of Paul Scofield, Irene Worth, and Alan Webb. As a work of art, it communicates vividly what great actors and a great director thought about Shakespeare's play as the 1960s drew to a close. Nihilistic, bleak, hopeless, ugly, full of horror and lacking pity, like Picasso's *Guernica* the terror of modern times is the subject, and Brook's film has used Shakespeare as the medium. Whether the film expresses Shakespeare's intent or not is a question beside the point. If the audience is to be the judge, then whether the brutal, chilling, *Lear* embodied by the film is now true, was true for the 1960s, or will become true tomorrow depends on how we see our world. If indeed what Brook saw in *Lear* is a troubling reminder of the despair and anger of the 1960s, then what will we make of the film and the play as the population ages in the next century? Preceded by the sentimental, almost pastoral *Lear* of Charles Laughton at Stratford, and followed by Kurosawa's reworking of the play in *Ran*, Peter Brook's film *King Lear* reminds us that, as modern editors have argued, *Lear* is not one, but many texts, not one play but multitudes. History will decide. It will be harsh, if what Peter Brook saw in Shakespeare's *Lear* proves to have been right.

Whether or not Peter Brook's *Lear* endures as an interpretation of the play, it nevertheless highlights a central aesthetic issue that Shakespeare on screen has brought to the fore. When is a performance of Shakespeare's play the play itself, and when is it an interpretation? Many theatre artists would argue that a play exists only when it is performed, and that any performance must be an interpretation, the sum of myriad artistic choices. The play on the page is as lifeless as a musical score; both await performance. And some literary critics concur. Indeed, the editors who seek to elucidate distinct '*Lears*' from early texts point to the revisions and alterations as responses to evolution in performance.

On the contrary, other literary critics agree with Charles Lamb that the theatre can stage only 'incomplete' *Lears*, the complete play being a literary artifact to be found in true and complete form only in the words of the text. Over the centuries, this argument runs, the theatre has again and again reformed and reinterpreted Shakespeare's plays, 'adapting' them, in the view of literary critics who denounced such 'distortions'. Or, to take the theatre artist's side, editors and literary critics have been writing about a dead play that has life only in their imaginations, untested by the realities of performance. Attempting to recover the original Globe staging only obscures the fact that the theatre lives in the present – the Globe's audiences can never be revived. However accurately one might restage the Globe *Lear*, one can never make up for the loss of Shakespeare's original audience. In this light, Shakespeare on screen is the most recent in the long evolution of Shakespeare under different theatre conventions.

Having taken form first as a stage performance and then as a film, Brook's *Lear* ties into this longstanding debate in an unusual way. Brook's *Lear* onstage follows the paradigm of high modernism in Shakespeare production: full text, a production unified by a 'concept' expressed in sets, costumes, and direction. Brook's Lear on film follows the same paradigm – yet it recognizes that, to realize the director's 'concept' in cinematic terms, one needs to rearrange and reinterpret the text. Come at the play from a foreign culture, as Kurosawa did (and in some ways as Brook, the expatriate did), and one sees a text that must be reworked if one is to perform the play truly. Here the word 'truly' divides critics into those who see textual accuracy as the touchstone and those who see it as subordinate to the creation of a performance that evokes a full tragic response from the audience, recognizing that the means to such a response will change from one theatre, one era and one culture to others. This latter 'multivariant' Shakespeare, as it might be called, conceives of '*Lear*' as a platonic ideal that may take an infinite number of actual shapes, one category being the various texts in various editions, others being different productions in different performance media, still others, translations verbal and theatrical into different cultures. In this view, each manifestation may be 'authentic' in its own terms, but not across media. Thus a text lacks the performance dimension entirely, yet it is still '*Lear*'; a performance in the theatre may omit parts of the text to make a unified performance; and a performance in the cinema, responding to different conventions, will recast the text yet more. So too, *Lear* in Japan and in Japanese theatre will transform the text even further.

To the old question, where does 'true' performance end and adaptation begin, one is tempted to answer with another: Who can say what the essence of this or any other Shakespeare play is? Many strive; when audiences respond, as they did to Brook's *Lear*, it behooves scholars and critics to examine what was done and to elucidate the means. Accordingly, we may know Shakespeare's play in its many forms still better.

NOTES

1. For a concise account of Brook's early career, see Daniel B. Pollack, 'Peter Brook: A Study of Modern Elizabethan and His Search for New Theatrical Forms', *DAI*, 34 (1973), 447-A.

2. In the 1959 production, at the Shakespeare Memorial Theatre, Stratford-upon-Avon, the director Glen Byam Shaw and the design team Motley created a bucolic milieu, and Laughton played a 'Father Christmas' Lear. To many critics it merely proved once again the play's unactability.

3. This description of the performance and those which follow are based upon theatre reviews and promptbooks kept in the Shakespeare Centre Library, Stratford-upon-Avon. A microfilm copy of these materials is kept at the University of Illinois Library. For helping me to prepare this paper, I am deeply grateful to my student Suzy L. Brandt, especially for her expert transcription of the film dialogue from the soundtrack.

4. In a later interview, Brook acknowledged these influences, especially Kott's, but insisted that by no means had he based the production on them. 'When you begin to say we do it in the style of a Beckett play, it's almost like saying Beckett wrote Shakespeare! ... Both Beckett and Brecht are incorporated in Shakespeare.... Though they are great figures of our time, they are minute figures compared to Shakespeare.' Quoted by Daniel Labielle, 'The Formless Hunch: An Interview with Peter Brook', *Modern Drama*, 28 (1980), 221-22. Kott's *Shakespeare Our Contemporary*, first published in French translation in 1961, appeared in English in 1966 with a preface by Brook.

5. *King Lear in Our Time* (London: Methuen, 1966), pp. 30-32.
6. *Shakespeare and the Film* (New York: Praeger, 1971), pp. 133-52.
7. Jack Jorgens, *Shakespeare on Film* (Bloomington: Indiana Univ. Press, 1977), p. 331n reports that microfilm copies of these draft scripts are now kept in at the Folger Shakespeare Library in Washington, D.C. For Jorgens' description and analysis of the film, see pp. 235-51 in the aforementioned book.
8. John Simon in the *New York Times* (19 December 1971), among others, complained bitterly that what was left was neither tragedy nor – as it lacked humor – absurdist drama. 'With such a Lear, no heights, no depths, merely, as Brook wants it, an absurd, godless, ridiculous universe, mindlessly grinding down motes into yet more insignificant motes. And why not so? Because the text, as written, is a tragedy, and unlike Beckett's gallows humor, contradicts Brook's vision of cosmic puniness.' Vincent Canby (*New York Times*, 23 November 1971), calling it 'a King Lear of splendor and shock', respectfully termed the film 'Mr. Brook's adaptation'. For a detailed run-down on the film's critical reception, see *Film Facts*, 14 (1971), pp. 685-89.
9. In an analysis of the film, Lillian Wilds, 'One *King Lear* for Our Time: A Bleak Film Vision by Peter Brook', *Literature/Film Quarterly*, 4, No. 2 (1976), pp.159-64, rightly points out that Brook's cuts on the text eliminate any touches of humanity in the play, thereby further emphasizing its cruelty. In her article Wilds argues persuasively for the unity of intention behind the film.
10. Quoted by Geoffrey Reeves in 'Finding Shakespeare on Film: From an Interview with Peter Brook', *Focus on Shakespearean Film*, ed. Charles Eckert (Englewood Cliffs: Prentice Hall, 1971), pp. 37-41, first published in *TDR*, 11 (1966).
11. 'Stream of consciousness' is too placid an expression for Brook's kaleidoscopic roller-coaster of images, an attempt to transmute verbal imagery into visual images which only demonstrates the medium's limitations. On the line 'poor naked wretches', for example, we see a pack of drowned rats, belly-up in the rain, and, as we do throughout the sequence, we wonder 'What *is* that? What's happening?' One can appreciate the intention, but the result is a disaster.
12. Jack Jorgens ponts out in a teaching manual of the film prepared for Audio Brandon films that in an early draft of the shooting script, Brook had contemplated a somewhat less abrupt opening: '"LEAR. Give me the map, Gloucester brings it to him. For a moment, we see side by side the two aged heads; both in their eighties, Gloucester fussy, anxious, and Lear, powerful, set. Lear unrolls the map as he looks around the room." And the scene begins.'
13. 'Lear Log', *TDR*, 8 (1963), pp. 103-21.
14. Labielle, p. 220.

Visible Darkness: Shakespeare's *King Lear* and Kurosawa's *Ran*

Ib Johansen

Raise your hand in the evening light
and watch it until it becomes transparent
and you see the sky and the trees through it.

Yoko Ono: 'Hand Piece' (1961)

Edg. Fraterretto cals me, and tells me *Nero* is an Angler in the Lake of Darknesse: pray
Innocent, and beware the foule Fiend.

Shakespeare: *King Lear* (F, III.6.2004-06)

The Lear Story

The archetypal plot in Shakespeare's *King Lear* (written some time between
1604 and 1606) – comprising the love-trial, the story of the King's three
daughters, etc. – bears a striking resemblance to motifs and narrative elements
to be found in a number of well-known traditional folk tales. Thus Lear's
youngest daughter Cordelia reminds us of Cinderella, and her situation is also
similar to that of the heroine of the British fairy tale 'Cap O'Rushes', where
'a very rich gentleman' expels his third daughter on account of an unsatis-
factory answer in a 'love-test', analogous to the one in Shakespeare's tragedy:

> So he says to the third, 'How much do *you* love me, my dear?' 'Why,' says she, 'I love
> you as fresh meat loves salt,' says she. Well, he were that angry. 'You don't love me at
> all,' says he, 'and in my house you stay no more.' So he drove her out there and then,
> and shut the door in her face.[1]

In one of Grimm's *Märchen*, 'The Goose-Girl at the Well' ('Die Gänsehirtin
am Brunnen'), a King likewise banishes his daughter in order to punish her for
comparing her love for him with her appreciation of salt; he divides his kingdom between the two elder daughters, 'but the youngest, with a sack of salt

tied to her back, was led into the wild forest by two servants and left there alone'.[2] In Grimm's tale the youngest daughter is taken into the household of a benevolent witch residing in the forest, and her parents do not succeed in finding her until a young count presents the Queen with 'a small box, carved out of an emerald', given to him by the witch as a reward for his services.[3] All the tears shed by the princess become precious pearls, and one of these pearls is in the box, enabling the King and Queen to discover her whereabouts, and soon afterwards the parents are reunited with their lost daughter.

In the fairy tales *salt* is represented as something apparently worthless, but in actual fact indispensable. In Shakespeare's *King Lear* Cordelia's fatal 'Nothing' (F, I.1.95) plays a similar role – an object is thus supplanted by a word (!) – and on a metaphorical level her *tears* also seem to possess miraculous qualities: in Act IV, Scene 3, Cordelia invokes the healing power of these self-same tears:

Cord. All blest Secrets,
All you vnpublish'd Vertues of the earth
Spring with my teares; be aydant and remediate
In the Goodman's desires... [distress, Q] (F, IV.3.2366-69).

In *King Lear*, however, all the wondrous events taking place in the fourth act (the reconciliation of Lear and Cordelia, the serenity of the King's mental state at the end of the act, etc.) are later annulled by the disastrous sequence of happenings in the last act – but that is another story!

The family saga of Lear and his three daughters belongs to Britain's remote and legendary past – to a pre-Christian as well as pre-Roman era. From Geoffrey of Monmouth's epoch-making *Historia Regum Britanniae* (*History of the Kings of Britain*), completed not later than 1138-39, up to the chronicles of the sixteenth century, a number of British histories reiterated more or less identical versions of the story, and it had thus been transmitted over a period of several centuries, before it was turned into a play by Shakespeare at the beginning of the seventeenth century. Whereas the account of Lear himself is provided with a happy ending in Geoffrey of Monmouth's *Historia* as well as in the versions of his followers, the story of Cordelia after her father's death is submitted to a tragic turn, insofar as she is taken prisoner by her two nephews and hangs herself in prison – thus the sequel to the Lear story proper may be said to justify Shakespeare's revision of the original plot in his *tragedy*.[4]

In Geoffrey of Monmouth's narrative as well as in later versions a feudal *ethos* seems to dominate the account: we are confronted with a story about filial ingratitude (Goneril, Regan) as well as 'natural' virtue (Cordelia), and Lear's trials and tribulations may be regarded as being linked up with his own *hamartia* or *hubris* (in Geoffrey of Monmouth's *Historia* Lear's father Bladud, like his predecessor Icarus, 'had fashioned him wings and tried to go upon the top of the air, when he fell upon the temple of Apollo in the city of London, and was dashed into many pieces'!).[5] Just as it is the case in Shakespeare's tragedy, Lear's dwindling retinue already in Geoffrey of Monmouth's version seems to reflect on or imperil the whole feudal system of values: without his noble entourage the ruler has somehow lost his 'aura' or maybe even his *essence*.[6] In a number of medieval versions of the Lear story it was submitted to an explicitly Christian (re)interpretation – it was *moralized* or *allegorized* for the benefit of pious believers, i.e. its truth-value (or use-value) as an edifying *exemplum* was emphasized by clerical exegetes. The story of Lear thus makes its appearance in three manuscript versions of the *Gesta Romanorum* (collected about the end of the thirteenth century),[7] and at the end of the fifteenth century it was incorporated into 'a Latin homily-book with a second part, a Promptuary, or repository of examples for composing sermons' (Perrett).[8] This book was written about 1470 by a Dominican friar of Basle by the name of Johannes Herolt, in Latin simply *Discipulus*. The *exemplum* may be translated as follows:

The Faithlessness of the World and Blood-Relations

You may read in the histories of the Britons that there was in Great Britain, before the time of the incarnation of the Lord, a certain [king] by the name of Keyr [sic!], who had three daughters. And when he asked the eldest one if she loved him dearly, she said that she loved him above anything else, and the king gave her in marriage, and he endowed her with a very large part of his kingdom to be possessed by her after his death. He asked the second daughter the same question, and he did to her as he had done to the first. But the third and youngest daughter said to him: Father, as much as you have, thus much are you worth, and I love you as much as you are worth and no more. But the indignant father was less fond of her than of the others and took less care of her, and he swore that he would give her no part of his land, but the king of the country called France took her as his wife on account of her virtuous behaviour and her beauty. But when enemies attacked the forementioned Keyr, he handed over his country to his two eldest daughters and their husbands, and they promised to treat him with respect and to carry out his will before anything else. However, when his country had been looted, and after he had been expelled by the eldest daughters, he was honourably received by the third daughter and her husband, and by means of their assistance he managed to regain his heritage, and after having disinherited the others, he gave it up for the benefit of his youngest daughter.
 The first daughter is the love and trust man assigns to worldly matters. The second daughter is the love and trust man assigns to his blood-relations. The third one is the love and trust man assigns to the works of mercy.[9]

In Johannes Herolt's version of the Lear (Leir, Keyr) story the didactic purpose of the tale tends to overshadow everything else. The moral is pointed out explicitly at the end of the story – this part of a medieval *exemplum* is called the *significatio* – and the spiritual lesson cannot possibly be overlooked. The allegorical significance seems to have done away with or supplanted the narrative 'kernel': in this case the message certainly threatens to root out the *medium*!

Even after the seventeenth century the Lear story has had a long afterlife, undergoing new elaborations and new interpretations in a novel like Balzac's *Père Goriot* (1834) or in such a modern version of the play as Edward Bond's *Lear* (1972). Like Peter Brook's film *King Lear* (1971) Bond's drama, depicting an extremely violent society dominated by a military logic and based on 'a pyramid of aggression' (Bond),[10] is obviously inspired by the Polish critic Jan Kott's reading of *King Lear* in the essay '"King Lear", or Endgame' in *Shakespeare Our Contemporary* (1964), where he emphasizes the grotesque and absurd (or 'absurdistic') elements in the play; and the violation of the classical code of the tragic genre is synonymous with a transformation of the absolute 'into a blind mechanism, a kind of automaton'.[11] We shall later return to these attempts to come to terms with Shakespeare's tragedy in the light of typically *modern* experiences and start by paying attention to the text (i.e. Shakespeare's play) 'itself'. In this connection the question of *genre* seems to be all-important. To what extent is it possible to read the text as an allegory? Where does the allegorical pattern break down in order to foreground other systems of signs, another *semiosis*?

From allegory to grotesque – the question of genre in *King Lear*

In *King Lear* the most clear-cut references to the allegorical tradition are to be found in the first and fourth acts. In the opening scene of the play the allegorical pattern is rather conspicuous in the abdication scene and the love-trial, where Lear subordinates his daughters to a 'test' in order to be able to evaluate their (degree of) love for him: 'Which of you shall we say doth loue vs most,/ That we, our largest bountie may extend/ Where Nature doth with merit challenge ...' (F, I.1.56-58). The opening of the tragedy is characterized by its solemnly ritualistic quality, by the fact that a high degree of ceremonial and rhetorical gravity qualifies the oonduct of the characters. On one level of meaning, this ritualistic overture may be linked up with the *representative* function of the royal protagonist, i.e. with Lear's position as a feudal monarch. According to William Frost, 'Ritual has these characteristics at least: it is ordinarily *public*, it is deliberate, and it is presumed to be predictable, in outline if not in detail'.[12] Jurgen Habermas has stressed the symbolic status of the noble caste (the power elite) in a feudal or late-feudal society, where the public sphere is connected with the representative function of the upper strata of the hierarchical system: 'The spectacular display of the representative public sphere is linked up with personal attributes: with ensigns (emblems, weapons), outward appearance (garments, hairstyle), gestures (salutations, bearing), and rhetoric (style of address, formal speech as such), in short, with a rigorous code associated with "noble" behaviour'.[13] All these characteristics fit in very well with Lear's symbolic position in the first Act, first Scene, where he is identified by means of his attributes: (1) his coat-of-arms (cf. the emblematic function of the dragon image in Lear's 'Come not betweene the Dragon and his wrath', F, I.1.130), (2) his coronet ('This Coronet part betweene you'), (3) his formal style of address vis-à-vis the other characters (his three daughters, Burgundy and France, etc., etc.), and finally (4) the rhetorical code he has adopted in his official speeches. The high style taken up in the abdication scene and the love-trial is also closely linked to the allegorical bias of the whole episode, i.e. to the fact that the characters tend to stand for (more or less) abstract political or ethical values, virtues and vices, etc.

In a certain sense the characters seem to take part in a kind of *tableau vivant*, and their position appears to be similar to that of puppets or automata performing a ritual (cf. Kent on Oswald taking 'Vanitie the puppets part' (V,F, II.2.1109)). Kent stresses this aspect of the abdication scene when he upbraids Lear for his behaviour towards his daughter(s): 'What wilt thou doe ould man, think'st thou that *dutie*/ Shall haue dread to speake, when *power* to *flatterie* bowes,/ To plainnes *honours* bound when *Maiesty* stoops to *folly*' (Q, I.1.148-50, my italics). In this passage allegorical values are ascribed to all the major characters in the love-trial: 'power' or 'Maiesty' is Lear, 'dutie' or 'honour' is Kent, 'flatterie' is Goneril and Regan, 'plainnes' is Cordelia, etc., etc. Even the word 'folly' may contain an oblique, anticipatory reference to the omnipresence of the Fool in the following scenes of the play (on one level of meaning the Fool may be regarded as a kind of externalization of Lear's 'foolishness').

Gradually this didactic or allegorical pattern breaks down; it becomes more and more difficult to determine the moral position of the characters in an unequivocal way. Not only are the main characters – and in particular Lear and Gloucester – submitted to a kind of carnivalistic 'uncrowning', but the theme of madness, dominating the third and fourth acts of the tragedy, also contributes to this epistemological disarray. Even in the middle acts of the play there are attempts to 'anchor' language – represented by the speeches of the main characters – in a kind of allegorical discourse, but somehow this discourse continually seems to miss the mark. The characters have lost control of the 'floating' signifiers. Edgar's raving homiletic style in his mad speeches as Bedlam beggar exemplifies this trend, and at the same time a number of scenes also take on a more or less overtly *parabolic* character: the Dover scene (IV.6) and Lear's reconciliation with Cordelia (IV.7) certainly have such overtones. However, the doctrinal point is getting out of hand in these scenes – in a sense there is a discrepancy between tenor and vehicle, and the episodes have become a sort of *Lehrstücke ohne Lehre*.

In the fourth Act, first Scene, Gloucester tries to summarize the 'lesson' of his unhappy situation after he has decided to let the Bedlam beggar (his own son Edgar in disguise) act as his guide on his way towards Dover: '*Glou.* 'Tis the times plague,/ When Madmen leade the blinde...' (F, IV.1.2234-35). The passage echoes one of Christ's parables in Luke 6.39: 'And he spake a parable unto them, Can the blind lead the blind? Shall they not both fall into the ditch?'. Actually, the fake madman (Edgar) leads his father to the very verge of an imaginary cliff and makes him think he throws himself out from the top of it – in a sense he falls into the ditch, but in another sense he is 'saved' through the benevolent intervention of his son, for the cliff is only there in his (Gloucester's) mind and they are treading even ground all the time. In the Dover scene the heights and the depths are purely imaginary. Or to put in another way: they are anchored in language and nowhere else.

The transformation of allegory in the sixteenth and seventeenth centuries into a system of signs no longer based on 'a strong idea of the divine transcendence' leads to a kind of epistemological crisis, where what Eco has labelled 'Hermetic drift' to a larger and larger extent commands the arena; 'Hermetic drift' is Eco's term for 'the interpretive habit which dominated Renaissance Hermetism and which is based on the principles of universal analogy and sympathy, according to which every item of the furniture of the world is linked to every other element (or to many) of this sublunar world and to every element (or to many) of the superior world by means of similitudes and resemblances'.[14] Everything reminds the educated Renaissance spectator of everything else, and it becomes virtually impossible to *anchor* the interpretive drift – it has become a kind of *semiosis run wild*.

According to Michel Foucault, what is characteristic of Renaissance semiosis – to use Eco's and Peirce's term slightly out of context – is 'a proliferation of meaning, ... a self-multiplication of signification, weaving relationships so numerous, so intertwined, so rich, that they can no longer be deciphered except in the esoterism of knowledge. Things themselves become so burdened with attributes, signs, allusions that they finally lose their own form'.[15] Michel Foucault regards this change of paradigm in Renaissance hermeneutics, resulting in a veritable *embarras de richesse*, as related to the changing position of *madness* in sixteenth- and seventeenth-century Europe: 'Freed from wisdom and from the teaching that organized it, the image begins to gravitate about its own madness'.[16] This point is certainly relevant in connection with *King Lear*, where Lear, the Fool, and Edgar as Tom o'Bedlam are all of them imbued with the spirit of such a semiotic 'drift', where 'the image begins to gravitate about its own madness'. Insofar as Edgar fulfills the role of a psychopomp (a spiritual 'guide') *vis-à-vis* his blind father, leading him towards the white cliffs of Dover in an attempt to 'save' him, his key-position with regard to the semiotic revolution carried out in the middle acts of the tragedy becomes apparent. But ''Tis the times plague,/ When Madmen leade the blinde', and even if Edgar stresses his own *therapeutic* aim in the Dover scene – letting his father jump from a non-existent cliff – it is also obvious that the salvatory scheme cannot possibly be controlled by the human agents: in the end Dover does not mean salvation, for Cordelia's forces are defeated in the decisive battle, leading to Cordelia's, Gloucester's as well as Lear's own death in the end. According to Edgar, 'Why I do trifle thus with his dispaire,/ Is done to cure it' (F, IV.6.2471-72), but in the ensuing episode, i.e. after his father's failed suicide attempt, he changes his protean identity once more, assuming the 'shape' of a simple countryman, but referring to his former status as that of a *devil* rather than a *beggar*:

> *Edg.* As I stood here below, me thought his eyes
> Were two full Moones: he had a thousand Noses,
> Hornes wealk'd, and waued like the enraged Sea:
> It was some Fiend: Therefore thou happy Father,
> Thinke that the cleerest Gods, who make them Honors
> Of mens Impossibilities, haue preserued thee.   (F, IV.6.2514-19).

At this point Edgar makes his father reenact another biblical scene, i.e. that of Christ's second temptation, where he is 'set on a pinnacle of the temple' (Matthew 4.5), and the tempter 'saith unto him, If thou be the Son of God, cast thyself down: for it is written, He shall give his angels charge concerning thee: and in *their* hands they shall bear thee up, lest at any time thou dash thy foot against a stone' (Matthew 4.6). Of course, Gloucester's attempted suicide is rather a *counter*-example, for he does *not* withstand the 'Fiend's' temptation, and his rescue does not depend on his personal merits, but on his son's ingenious stratagem – and in this situation his son is both a demonic agent and a spiritual aid, i.e. the whole episode is open to widely different (and even self-contradictory) interpretations.

The 'Fiend' with his 'thousand noses', eyes appearing like 'two full Moones', and strange 'Hornes', belongs to the realm of the grotesque – somehow his demonic appearance is overdone or overblown, and only the superstitious Gloucester is capable of being taken in by Edgar's account.[17] According to Jan Kott, *King Lear* is characterized by its 'philosophical cruelty', and Kott stresses the *grotesque* quality of the drama, comparing its *ethos* to that of the new theatre (Brecht, Dürrenmatt, Beckett, et al.): 'In this new theatre there are no characters, and the tragic element has been superseded by the grotesque. The grotesque is more cruel than tragedy'.[18] In Jan Kott's view, this might also be a definition of Shakespeare's poetic code in *King Lear*.[19] Anyway, Edgar's *maneristic* portrait of the imaginary devil definitely reminds us of Arcimboldo and other Renaissance painters using emphatically grotesque pictorial effects in their canvases.[20] Furthermore, what is characteristic of the Renaissance groteque is precisely the way in which human and non-human (e.g. animal or vegetable) forms are intermingled, and this is what happens in Edgar's description of a composite fiend, where the macrocosm (the moon and the sea) contributes to the *monstrosity* of the supernatural being. The physical peculiarities of the devil in Edgar's harangue quoted above recall Mikhail Bakhtin's characterization of 'the grotesque image of the body' in folk culture in his book on Rabelais:

> ...the artistic logic of the grotesque image ignores the closed, smooth, and impenetrable surface of the body and retains only its excrescences (sprouts, buds) and orifices, only that which leads beyond the body's limited space or into the body's depths. Mountains and abysses, such is the relief of the grotesque body; or speaking in architectural terms, towers and subterranean passages.[22]

In the Dover scene the imaginary landscape is literally *incorporated* into the grotesque image of the physical appearance of the fiend, and the borderline between body and world seems to be blurred or non-existent.

In the fourth act of the play the theme of love (cf. the love-trial of the first Act, first Scene) and the theme of madness converge, and this catachrestic collision between diametrically opposed motifs contributes to the semiotic revolution hinted at above. The allegorical plot is more or less absorbed by the grotesque imagery, but at the same time it is still possible to discern traces of an allegorical structure beneath the sound and fury of orchestrated madness in the middle acts. Thus the pessimistic reference to madmen leading the blind (cf. above) may be linked up with a passage where Lear calls Gloucester 'blinde Cupid' (F, IV.6.2581). Actually, the symbolic connotations of the fourth act point in the direction of a text by the French poet Louise Labé, translated into English by Robert Greene as *The Debate Betweene Follie and Loue* (1587), where Folly puts out Cupid's eyes, but is later commanded by Jupiter to 'guide and conduct blinde Loue whether she seemeth best'.[23] This is a fairly accurate description of Edgar's role *vis-à-vis* his blind father (*alias* Cupid), and actually Gloucester himself seems to be dimly aware of a kind of poetic justice involved in his tragic destiny when he finally realizes that his own 'follies' have led him to this impasse (i.e. the scene where he is blinded): '*Glou.* O my Follies! Then Edgar was abus'd,/ Kinde Gods, forgiue me that, and prosper him' (F, III.7.2168-69). And in the last act Edgar summarizes the outcome of Gloucester's adultery in the following way:

The Gods are iust, and of our pleasant vices
Make instruments to plague vs:
The darke and vitious place where thee he got,
Cost him his eyes. (F, V.3.3131-34)

In Thomasin von Zerclaere's didactic poem 'Der Wälsche Gast' (written around 1215), Love says: 'I am blind and I make blind',[24] and Cupid's blindness is often moralized in medieval and Renaissance literature; Gloucester's want of sight thus readily suggests the powerful presence of the blind bow-boy in the sinister world of the play. In Act III, Scene 4, Edgar in his disguise as Bedlam beggar characterizes Gloucester – appearing with a torch in his hand – as a *demon* (actually one of the devils from Samuel Harsnett's polemical treatise):

> *Edg.* This is the foule Flibbertigibbet; he begins at Curfew, and walkes at first Cocke: Hee giues the Web and the Pin, squints the eye, and makes the Hare-lippe; Mildewes the white Wheate, and hurts the poore Creature of earth. (F, III.4.1895-99)

According to the Oxford English Dictionary a 'flibbertigibbet' can also be used about 'a flighty or frivolous woman', and the name that Edgar attaches to Gloucester is thus already in its common usage erotically coloured; in this passage Gloucester seems to make his appearance as a diabolised version of the classical god of love. Edgar is eager to stress the fact that the number of devils is infinite – and he comes up with one strange name after another for this infernal breed: 'The Prince of Darkenesse is a Gentleman. *Modo* he's call'd, and *Mahu*' (F, III.4.1921-22). The breakdown of medieval allegory as well as classical mythology apparently results in this disastrous proliferation of devils – and as long as the subject has not learned to come to terms with their strange nomenclature, there seems to be no great chance of conquering the omnipresent evil they represent.[25] Actually, the extravagant number of names signalizes a deep-rooted unease and estrangement from reality on the part of the speaking (counting) subject – trying one name after another in order to pinpoint an unnameable evil appears to be a rhetorical strategy adopted in a futile attempt to *control* the said evil. And the demon lover 'hurts the poore Creature of earth': the foule Flibbertigibbet 'giues the Web and the Pin, squints the eye', just as Thomas von Zerclaere's *Diu Minne* declares: '*Ich bin blint und mach blinten*'.[26]

Hyperbole and paradox – Renaissance wit and the rhetorical strategy of the play

The rhetorical language of Shakespeare's *King Lear* is dominated by two conflicting figures: on the one hand the *hyperbole*, on the other the *paradox*. In George Puttenham's *The Arte of English Poesie* (1589) hyperbole is called 'for his immoderate excesse ... the ouer reacher',[27] and this characterization fits in very well with King Lear's use of the figure:

> Blow windes, & crack your cheeks; Rage, blow
> You Cataracts, and Hyrricano's spout,
> Till you haue drench'd our Steeples, 'drown the Cockes... (F, III.2.1656-58)

The figure is thus governed by a principle of excess, and the passage quoted above certainly exemplifies what Thomas Nashe has called 'the swelling bumbast of bragging blanke verse'.[28] But at the same time it is obvious that in

King Lear this excess (literally) leads to 'nothing', and actually 'nothing' is one of the key-words of the text, from Lear's initial 'nothing can come of nothing' (Q, I.1.92) to all the reverberations effected by this 'annihilating' remark. The return to nothing involves a *paradoxical* situation where opposites meet: King and Fool, wise man and madman, culture and nature, all and nothing, etc., etc. But the point is precisely that it is impossible to get to the bottom of things. There is no end to human misery, as Edgar observes: 'And worse I may be yet: the worst is not,/ so long as we can say this is the worst' (F, IV.1.2210-11). Language turns out to be unable to cope with the human condition – there is an insurmountable gap between language and the 'real'.

In a certain sense this insight represents an oblique comment on the Renaissance concept of 'wit', for this notion actually implies that man *is* capable of mastering himself as well as the world (and other people) by linguistic means. In *King Lear* the bastard Edmund brags: 'Let me, if not by birth, haue lands *by wit,/* All with me's meete, that I can fashion fit' (F, I.2.503-04, my italics). During the Renaissance rhetoric tended to replace scholastic logic – or logic itself was 'rhetoricized' – which implied that what was important was no longer rigid semantic rules, but rather a certain nonchalance with regard to the relationship between language and 'truth'. This situation is accompanied by the decline of the feudal system and traditional aristocratic values. In England Lyly's *Euphues: The Anatomy of Wit* (1578) illustrates this development, 'the replacement of action by style', where 'the members of the remnant feudal aristocracy of the sixteenth century could show that they 'belonged' only by the complexity of their talk and the refinement of their manners and tastes'.[29] A typical Renaissance genre that demonstrates this emphasis on wit and rhetoric is precisely the *paradox*, a genre that was based on *the defense of contraries*, and where the aim is , in the words on the title-page of a typical collection of paradoxes, 'only to exercise yong wittes in difficult matters'.[30] In *King Lear* the Fool is the unequalled master of this rhetorical genre, and his virtuoso command of the said and other minor or 'gnomic' literary forms is obvious from the very outset (cf. his use of proverbs, rhymes, riddles, 'catechistic' dialogue, etc., etc.). When Lear himself takes over the role of the Fool in the middle acts of the play, he similarly adopts the Fool's linguistic habits, and the Fool's final exit in the third Act, sixth Scene, even submits the very notion of time (temporality itself) to a surprising paradoxical 'turn'. Both characters are caught up in a compulsion to repeat, to use the same rhetorical figure:

> *Lear.* Make no noise, make no noise, draw the Curtaines: so, so, wee'l go to Supper i' th' morning.
> *Foole.* And Ile go to bed at noone. (F, III.6.2041-43)

Certainly, the time is out of joint, and language is unable to cure the disease: it can only provide us with a painstaking diagnosis – or is it an autopsy?

Every inch a samurai – the Lear story and Kurosawa's *Ran*

In his long career as a film-maker the Japanese director Akira Kurosawa has twice been inspired by Shakespearean sources: in his *Throne of Blood* (*Kumonosu-Jo*, 1957), adapted from *Macbeth* (written between 1603 and 1606), and in his *Ran* (1985), loosely modelled on *King Lear*, but also influenced by Kurosawa's researches into medieval Japanese history. According to Stephen Prince in *The Warrior's Camera*. *The Cinema of Akira Kurosawa* (1991), in the case of the latter film the director 'became fascinated by a warlord reputed to have had three excellent sons and wondered what would have happened if the three had been, instead, bad. What happens is the destruction of their clan and domain, much as in *Kagemusha*'.[31] Thus *Ran*, like its Shakespearean model, seems to be based on an exemplary or 'archetypal' story, i.e. the story of the Japanese warlord and his sons, but like *King Lear* the film deviates in significant ways from its edifying source. For the film is very much coloured by the pessimistic – or even nihilistic – outlook characteristic of Kurosawa in his later films, at least up to *Dreams* (1990), for this film, on the other hand, seems to initiate a new 'turn' in Kurosawa's career as a director.[32]

In films like *Seven Samurai* (*Shichinin no samurai*, 1954) and *Yojimko* (1961) Kurosawa has contributed to a genre that is all-important in the history of the Japanese movie, i.e. *the samurai film*. In many respects the samurai film may be compared to the Hollywood western – adopting a number of the same narrative formulas and clichés as its American counterpart. Like the Western the samurai film is set in the past, and 'Both types of film are about men of violence who are defined in terms of their weapons ...' (Prince),[33] i.e. the gunfighter's display of his six-gun may be compared to the samurai's handling of his sword. Kurosawa is clearly indebted to the American Western, in particular to John Ford, but on the other hand Kurosawa also influenced Hollywood (cf. for example the Hollywood version of *Seven Samurai*, i.e. *The Magnificent Seven*, and a film like Peckinpah's *The Wild Bunch*). Kurosawa in his own way added a personal touch to the samurai film, and according to Alain Silver, the Japanese director right from his debut in 1943 with *Sanshiro Sugata* 'incorporated action scenes, humour, and an aggressive pictorialism into the standard and stable narrative formats of *jidai-geki* ['period drama'] and melodrama'.[34] Whereas Kurosawa is not as explicitly anti-feudal as for example Masaki Kobayashi in his *Hara-Kiri* (*Seppuku*, 1962), we find in Kurosawa's early films a strong element of social consciousness: 'In *Judo Saga* and *Seven Samurai* and, by opposing equation, in *Rashomon* and *Throne of Blood*, Kurosawa's characters survive or perish based in large part on their respect for the ethical values of society' (Alain Silver).[35] In *Yojimbo* the *ronin*, i.e. the disenfranchised or masterless samurai, is confronted with a thoroughly corrupt society, a village where wholesale slaughter is the order of the day, but even under these circumstances and even if his stance is grim and sardonic, he nevertheless sticks to his heroic role – and in the end he manages to overcome and/or outwit his opponents and put an end to the internecine feud between two families that has been going on for a very long time. Even though the heroic *ethos* is undercut by ironic reservations in Kurosawa's early period films, it is very much present as an active force within the filmic universe.

Throne of Blood is characterized by a much more gloomy perspective on human existence. The very landscapes of the film point in the direction of a kind of cosmic emptiness – a bleached sky, fog, and desolate plains provide the frame for a tale of ruthless ambition and violence. In a Kabuki-like chant at the beginning of the film the moral/religious 'message' is summarized for the spectators: 'A proud castle stood in this desolate place/ Its destiny wedded to a mortal's lust for power/ Here lived a warrior strong yet weakened by a woman/ Driven to add his tribute to the throne of blood/ The devil's path will always lead to doom.' Instead of Shakespeare's three witches or Weird Sisters there is only a solitary white-haired, almost transparent woman blocking the way of the two main characters (Washizu *alias* Macbeth and Miki *alias* Banquo), as they try to get back to the castle of their feudal lord after the victory at the beginning of the film. This woman is clearly a spirit and after having predicted the future destiny of the two warriors vanishes into thin air together with her cottage and spinning-wheel. In accordance with the tenets of Buddhism her emphasis is on the nothingness of human life and material existence: 'Men are vain mortals; life is but a thread...' Prince notices that the introspective elements in Shakespeare's *Macbeth* have been omitted in Kurosawa's *Trone of Blood*, i.e. such meditations on existential and moral issues as we find in the protagonist's great soliloquies in Shakespeare's play: 'Life's but a walking shadow; a poor player,/ That struts and frets his hour upon the stage,/ And then is heard no more...' (*Macbeth*, V.6.24-26).[36] Instead the emotions of the characters are externalized or turned into visible symbols, and Kurosawa also draws on the conventions of the traditional Noh theatre, where a high degree of stylization characterizes the performance of the players, all of them male – the white, mask-like appearance of Asaji's (Lady Macbeth's) face also points in the direction of the Noh style of acting. In an interview Kurosawa himself explains how he showed each of his actors in *Throne of Blood* a mask corresponding to his/her part in the film: 'To Isuzu Yamada who acted the role of Asaji I showed the mask named Shakumi. This was the mask of a beauty no longer young, and represented the image of a woman about to go mad ...' On the whole, 'The mask-like presentation of characters, the stylization of their movements (especially evident in Lady Asaji), and the elimination of verbal introspection, typical of the Noh, displace the emotions of the film onto objects and the environment' (Prince).[37]

A samurai must be willing to die for his master, and his loyalty towards his feudal lord is supposed to be absolute. But in *Throne of Blood* this feudal code has been supplanted by a deadly rivalry between master and liege, and it is stated twice in the film that 'Every samurai longs to be the master of a castle'. In this case the samurai (Washizu) can only gain power by murdering his master, and it turns out that Tsuzuki, the master of Cobweb Castle, possesses none of the meek, saintly qualities of the murdered Duncan in Shakespeare's *Macbeth:* he himself has only become master by killing *his* predecessor and supposedly this could go on forever. This might recall Jan Kott's Grand Mechanism in his essay on 'The Kings' in *Shakespeare Our Contemporary* (1964), a mechanism according to whose ruthless logic there are no longer good and bad kings, insofar as sovereignty is always based on violence, cruelty and treason, or 'A mechanism according to whose laws the road to power is at the same time the way to death ...'.[38] In *Throne of Blood* Lady Asaji similarly reminds her husband of the inexorable logic of the Grand Mechanism: 'Have you forgotten his Lordship killed his own master...'. The salvatory scheme of Shakespeare's *Macbeth* is thus deliberately downgraded in Kurosawa's film, insofar as (almost) all the characters are caught in the same web (narrative logic), represented on a visual level by the labyrinthine forest ('Cobweb Forest', described in the film as 'a natural labyrinth') as well as by the name of the main castle, *Cobweb* Castle. It is also significant that Washizu is finally killed by his *own* men, i.e. through yet another act of treason on their part – pierced by dozens and dozens of arrows like a veritable porcupine!

The code regulating samurai behaviour is summarized in the concept of *bushido*, 'the way of the warrior'. The term *bushido* was reputedly coined by a sage of the seventeenth century, Yamago Soko, but it must be stressed that it does not exist as an actual written record according to which a warrior should pattern his life.[39] It must also be emphasized that the samurai code is in many respects self-contradictory. Thus *giri*, comprising the duty or fealty which the individual warrior owes to his master, may sometimes collide with *ninjo*, the subjective or natural conscience of the samurai. The samurai may be compelled by his master to take part in an unjust feud against a rival clan or family,[40] and furthermore the ethical implications of the Buddhist creed, with its emphasis on the illusory character of the material world and human existence, may in some cases be in conflict with the samurai code or the samurai concept of honour.

Hidetora, the protagonist of Akira Kurosawa's *Ran* (1985), has been able to consolidate his power or sovereign position only by ruthlessly persecuting all those who opposed him – killing in the process his real and potential enemies without bothering very much about the moral implications of his behaviour. His long life has been an endless series of military campaigns and he has put to the sword not only his enemies, but also a number of those who trusted him or were unable to defend themselves against him. At the beginning of the film his status seems, in many respects, to be that of a bloodthirsty tyrant, and thus his position differs rather much from that of Lear, his counterpart in Shakespeare's play, characterizing himself in Act Three as 'a man,/ More sinn'd against, then sinning' (F, III.2.1712-13). His son Saburo, whose position is similar to that of Cordelia in Shakespeare's play, points out at the beginning of the play that giving up power must necessarily have disastrous consequences, considering Hidetora's former career as a merciless warlord: 'You have spilled so much human blood you cannot measure it. You have lived without mercy or pity. But Father, we, too, are children of this degraded age of strife; you do not know what we may be thinking – 'my dear children,' you think. To me, Father, you are none other than a madman – a senile old madman' (*Ran Screenplay*, p. 17). At this point Hidetora has just given up his absolute power, handing over the headship of the Ichimonji clan to his eldest son Taro and commanding his two other sons, Jiro and Saburo, to take over the Second and Third Castles 'and assist Taro, who will be in the First Castle' (*Ran Screenplay*, p. 13). Saburo foresees that eventually Hidetora's own sons, i.e. Taro and Jiro, will turn against their father, and this is precisely what happens in a bloody battle scene in the middle of the film, where all Hidetora's retainers are massacred in an attack on the Third Castle by Taro's and Jiro's troops. As in *Lear* Hidetora's abdication at the beginning of the film leads to a period with severe political unrest and civil war, and in the process Jiro even lets one of his clansmen, Kurogane, kill his brother Taro, so that he himself can take over the headship of the House of Ichimonji – the shot is fired during the attack on the Third Castle, and afterwards an enemy soldier is blamed for Taro's death ('He was shot by a soldier lying in ambush with a rifle near the watchtower on the outworks ...', *Ran Screenplay*, p. 50). In this context it might be interesting to notice that Jiro has many features in common with Edmund in *King Lear*. Like Edmund he despises the legal system that prevents him from taking up the position of his elder brother: 'Why should I have to spend my life groveling at my elder brother's feet just because I was born twelve months later? I will kick off these shackles' (*Ran Screenplay*, p. 32). Of course, this speech reminds us of Edmund's first soliloquy in Shakespeare's play:

> ... wherefore should I
> Stand in the plague of custome, and permit
> The curiosity of Nations, to depriue me?
> For that I am some twelue, or fourteene Moonshines
> Lag of a Brother? (F, I.2.336-40)

In many respects the classical samurai code seems to be no longer valid in Kurosawa's *Ran*: modern weapons (guns) have supplanted the traditional sword, the 'soul of the samurai',[41] and therefore the outcome of a war is no longer dependent on the prowess and swordsmanship of the individual warrior, insofar as victory has become the product of sheer force of arms; in Japan the battle of Sekigahara in 1600 marks the advent of this new age, and it is also about this time that many samurai or masterless swordsmen took up a much more mercenary view with regard to their profession (cf. the *ronin*'s negotiations with the two warring families in Kurosawa's *Yojimbo*). And just as Shakespeare's *King Lear*, in György Lukacs' phrase, may be read as a comment on 'the problematicalness and break-up of the feudal family',[42] the traditional Japanese notion of the all-importance of the *uji* or clan, with its emphasis on the family as the ethical centre, has been considerably weakened in *Ran*. The title of Kurosawa's film means 'chaos' in Japanese, and this is what the advent of 'modernity' in politics as well as individual life actually amounts to in *Ran*.

A world without gods

In his film adaptation of *King Lear* Kurosawa has made a number of significant changes: instead of three daughters, there are three sons, there is no formal subplot (the Gloucester story is left out), etc., etc. But on the other hand, many of the elements that have been omitted are reintroduced in a slightly different context. Thus one of the important scenes in *King Lear*, i.e. the blinding of Gloucester, *does* make its appearance in *Ran*, but here it is relegated to the past, and what is more important, it is Hidetora himself who has blinded a boy belonging to a rival clan – after having burned down his father's castle and massacred the rest of the family apart from his sister (she is married to Hidetora's son Jiro). In one of the most moving scenes in *Ran* Hidetora, who has fled from the burning castle after the attack (cf. above), encounters his former victim Tsurumaru in a straw hut in the middle of a violent storm (cf. Lear's encounter with the mad Bedlam beggar *alias* Edgar in Shakespeare's play). Tsurumaru tries to follow his sister's teachings, 'to pray to the Buddha and rid myself of hatred' (*Ran Screenplay*, p. 62). But he finds it very hard to live in accordance with his Buddhist belief and is quite unable to sleep peacefully at night. Like his sister Sue, however, Tsurumaru does represent a spiritual dimension strangely at odds with the norms and demands of 'this degraded age of strife' (Saburo) – and strangely at odds with Hidetora's relentless *Realpolitik* as well. Tsurumaru offers even his enemy his hospitality in his straw hut and plays the flute for him (in this connection it is worthwhile remembering that the flute is an important instrument in the Noh theatre). Later, when he and his sister Sue have to flee from their pursuers, he forgets to bring his flute with him, and Sue's attempt to get it back turns out to be fatal, for she is killed by an assassin – actually one of her own husband Jiro's men sent out to kill her because Jiro wants to marry Taro's widow Kaede. The latter's family has *also* been wiped out by Hidetora, but unlike Sue Kaede is unwilling to forget and forgive, and her vendetta against the whole Ichimonji clan in the end turns out to be successful: Kaede has demanded Sue's decapitation by Jiro before she is willing to become his wife, and her machinations are also behind the further disastrous course of events, eventually leading to the destruction of the rest of the clan, including Saburo and Hidetora.

In a certain sense it is *giri* or Kaede's sense of an obligation towards her murdered family that has resulted in the vendetta carried out against the whole Ichimonji clan. According to Alain Silver, 'The alternatives for the designated avenger or avengers were narrow: either seek out the man who has offended the *uji* and place his severed head on the tomb of the one he had caused to die to expiate that soul or suffer a loss of face which might well require self-immolation instead'.[43] Kaede, however, may be said to disregard the very norms behind this code of honour by including the innocent Sue in the whole-sale slaughter of the Ichimonji family. In many respects, her position in the film may be compared to that of Goneril and Regan in *King Lear* – and her function as a beautiful *femme fatale*, exerting her seductive power over her treacherous brother-in-law Jiro in order to make him subscribe to her plans, also recalls Lady Asaji's fatal influence on Washizu in *Throne of Blood*. Actually, her behaviour is in many ways just as stylized and ritualistic as that of Asaji. There is in particular a significant scene where she threatens and cuts her brother-in-law with a dagger, and where she handles her weapon with an almost choreographic precision. The first man (Kurogane) sent out to kill Sue finds the deed so 'unnatural' that he returns with a stone fox's head instead – implying in a mock-explanatory speech that Kaede is actually *a fox in disguise*, i.e. an evil demon. In this connection the Japanese spectator is undoubtedly aware of the symbolic position of such foxes disguised as women in traditional folklore, in fairy tales, etc. Foxes frequently appear as beautiful women and in many folk tales men are lured into marrying a *fox wife* – quite often her tail finally reveals her true identity, and then she has to leave her husband (cf. the folk legend 'The Fox Wife', where a farmer discovers a fox's tail hanging out of his wife's bed'; before leaving the farmer and their child she makes the rice-fields fruitful, and then 'In the darkness the fox-wife disappeared, rolling up the arrowroot leeaves scattered nearby. For that reason arrowroot leaves always show their undersides ...').[44] In *Ran* Kurosane makes jokes about Sue being 'a fox in disguise' (*Ran Screenplay*, p. 74), and then he goes on with a long rambling discourse on the numerous tricks of this crafty animal: 'Here in Japan, the fox served at court as Princess Tamano and worked even more treachery. It is said that she finally turned into a white fox with nine tails. After that there was no trace of the white fox. It is possible it might have settled around here. Be careful, my lord, be careful' (*Ran Screenplay*, p. 74). In *King Lear* Goneril is also compared to a fox in Act One, Scene Four, where the Fool makes oblique references to the hanging of Reynard the Fox: 'A Fox, when one has caught her,/ And such a Daughter,/ Sould sure to the Slaughter,/ If my Cap would buy a Halter,/ So the Fool follows after' (F, I.4.837-41).[45]

In the end, however, it is not the evil *femme fatale* (Kaede) who is beheaded in *Ran* but the innocent Sue, and the camera focuses on the corpses of two women resting on the grass and flowers of the field outside Tsurumaru's hut – Sue's lady-in-waiting and Sue herself: 'The young lady's [i.e. Sue's] neck is covered with a bundle of wild flowers which were picked by rough hands. ... The hand clasps Tsurumaru's flute – a sad and cruel sight' (*Ran Screenplay*, pp. 105-06). In this context the flute clearly represents the spirituality that is threatened and (perhaps definitively) defeated by the atrocious events of the film. After Saburo's and Hidetora's death the Fool (Kyoami) cries out his despair, but is upbraided by Tango (*alias* Kent, Hidetora's faithful retainer) for blaming the deity for human misdeeds (cf. Gloucester on humans as 'Flies', F, IV.1.2221-22):

KYOAMI
(Yelling)

Is there no God or Buddha in this world? Damnation! God and the Buddha are nothing but mischievous urchins! Are they so bored in Heaven that they enjoy watching men die like worms? Damn God! Is it so amusing to see and hear human beings cry and scream?

TANGO

Enough! Do not slander God or the Buddha! They are the ones who are crying!...
(*Ran Screenplay*, p. 99)

The old world is about to disintegrate: Tsurumaru has lost his flute, and after the attack on the Third Castle, when Hidetora tries to commit *hara-kiri* or *seppuku* in accorance with the samurai code, i.e. because it would be shameful to survive after all his men have been massacred, he finds out that he has no longer got his sword, i.e. he has actually lost the visible symbol of his status as a member of a privileged warrior caste. What is left at this point are desolate plains, the ruins of a castle Hidetora himself burned down to the ground, the open sky. This is the setting where the majority of the remaining scenes are shot (there are a great number of outdoor scenes in the film).

Like Lear's Fool Kyoami sticks to his master and tries to make him aware of his foolishness, and he, too, uses a paradoxical strategy in order to make his surroundings aware of the antinomies of human existence 'in this degraded age of strife' (Saburo). The role is played by Peter, a famous Japanese transvestite, and as has been observed by Dave Kehr, the Fool's freedom of movement – his freedom to jump and dance and gesticulate violently – is in sharp contrast with 'the slow, formal, Kabuki-like gestures' of the other actors.[46] Even if Kyoami is momentarily overcome by his emotions (cf. above), his attempts to conquer philosophical dualism and relativize intellectual categories may also remind us of the way of zen, where a difficult or impossible problem is often approached by means of paradoxical argumentation: '*At dusk the cock announces dawn;/ At midnight, the bright sun*' (cf. 'And Ile go to bed at noone',

F, III.6.2043). Kyoami is similarly aware of the relativity of madness and sanity in an age where everything is out of joint: 'In a mad world only the mad are sane' (*Ran*).

Kyoami (Peter) and Hidetora (Tatsuya Nakadai). In this comic sketch, incorporated into the opening scene of the film, Kyoami turns himself into a hare and moves about with great agility in front of his master.

In *Throne of Blood* even the scenes that take place in the daytime are imbued with a ghostly, sinister and nocturnal quality; Kurosawa uses the black-and-white film medium very efficiently to convey an overall impression of 'preternaturalness', of impenetrable mystery. In the colour film *Ran* there is very little camera movement, and even when Kurosawa shoots the attack on the Third Castle, he places the camera 'above the battle, looking down with serene detachment on the columns of archers and horse-men as they charge in geometrical precision' (Kehr).[48] The claustrophobic sense of space in *Throne of Blood* is superseded by the panoramic vistas and wide-open exteriors of *Ran*. Very often the figures are almost dwarfed by their surroundings – or they are deliberately placed in the immediate vicinity of the picture frame (cf. for instance, Hidetora's encounter with Sue, Jiro's wife, where both figures are placed very close to the margin of the picture, in accordance with the principles of *sumi-e* composition in Japanese pictorial art: 'The composition of leaving a large area white and drawing persons and things only within a limited section of the space is peculiar to Japanese art ...' (Kurosawa).[49] In *Ran*

the characters in many scenes tend to be reduced to nothing by their impressive surroundings – by the wide-open, 'sublime' spaces of the film. The
tragic implications of this situation are suggested by Prince in his sensitive
rendering of the very last shots of the movie:

> Standing on the wall of [the ruined castle], etched against the horizon, Tsurumaru
> advances toward the edge of a precipice, feeling his way with a cane. Suddenly, he loses
> his balance and drops the image of Buddha he has faithfully carried. Kurosawa then cuts
> to an extreme long shot to offer the final image: a blind man at the edge of a precipice,
> bereft of his god, alone in a darkening world.[50]

Actually, the camera lense *also* focuses on the image of the Buddha, bereft
of its faithful adherent (Tsurumaru), so that the isolation and defeat of man
and god is reciprocal, as it were. An enormous distance may be said to separ-
ate this final image of man in a world without gods and its counterpart in
Shakespeare's *King Lear*, i.e. the parabolic Dover Scene, where the protagonist
(Gloucester) is still provided with *some* kind of guide or psychopomp, even if
''Tis the times plague,/ When Madmen leade the blinde ...' (F, IV.1.2234-35).
In *Ran* the hidden god remains permanently out of reach – in this symbolic
Untergang des Morgenlandes or twilight of the Empire of the Sun what is left
is visible darkness: *'At dusk the cock announces dawn;/ At midnight, the bright
sun.'*

In *The Bottom Translation* (1987) Jan Kott stresses the importance of the
landscape in film versions of *King Lear*: 'In even the most illusionistic scen-
ography, the decorations in the theater are always conventional. In the film, the
landscape is real. Of all the royal tragedies, *King Lear* probably most needs a
real landscape.'[51] Just as Peter Brook transferred the plot of the play to 'the
cold landscape of Jutland' and the Russian director Grigori Kozintsev 'took his
Lear into the Russian steppe ... Kurosowa took his *Lear* into medieval
Japan'.[52] Furthermore, in *Ran* he

> trims the plot to the bone. Hidetora's three sons are all that remains of Lear's three
> daughters and Gloucester's two sons. Shakespeare had doubled the plot of the old folk
> tale about three daughters (two vile and one noble): Kurosawa has cut and compressed
> it.[53]

Jan Kott stresses the apocalyptic quality of Kurosawa's *Ran* – a quality that
emerges in particular in the battle scenes of the film: 'Kurosawa is the distinct
and peerless master of battle scenes. Even the cruelest of them makes you gasp
in amazement. They are a vision of the Apocalypse rendered with the highest
artistic perfection.'[54]

Jan Kott's reading of *Ran* is in accordance with his *modernist* approach to
universal history, his emphasis on the essentially *sterile* character of the landscapes in which human beings tend to find themselves in contemporary cul-

Preparing for the battle. Jiro's and Saburo's armies in front of the wood.

ture. As a matter of fact, the subject is confronted with a cosmos characterized by its 'empty transcendence' or 'empty ideality' (Hugo Friedrich),[55] and Kott interprets the final shots of the film precisely in terms of such a universal nothingness (cf. also Prince's reading of the ending of the film):

> The blind man feels his way to the edge of the abyss. The parchment falls from his hands and unrolls over the bluff where the wind gently rocks the likeness of the smiling Buddha. The sky is light blue, streaked with gentle, slow-moving clouds. The blue sky is completely empty.[56]

Kurosawa's filmic *Götterdämmerung* certainly makes it relevant to (re)read Japanese as well as global history in this way. But Kurosawa's later films remind us that perhaps the warring universals – heaven and earth, dream and reality, childhood and old age, etc., etc. – may come together and even get on speaking terms with each other in a less destructive fashion. Until the end of the world – and even afterwards (?) – *ripeness is all!*

Notes

Works cited (abbreviated titles): Q = William Shakespeare: *King Lear, 1608 (Pied Bull Quarto)*. Shakespeare Quarto Facsimiles, No. 1 (Oxford: At the Clarendon Press, 1964). F = *The Norton Facsimile. The First Folio of Shakespeare*, Prepared by Charlton Hinman (New York: W.W. Norton & Company, Inc., 1968). A reprint of the First Folio (1623). *Ran Screenplay = Ran*. Illustrations by Akira Kurosawa. Screenplay by Akira Kurosawa, Hideo Oguni, Ide Masato. Translated by Tadashi Shishido (Boston & London: Shambhala, 1986). *Ran = Ran*, 1992 Foxvideo, Inc. I have also made use of *Throne of Blood*, Connoisseur Video CR 043.

1. Katharine M. Briggs (ed.): *British Folk Tales and Legends: A Sampler* (London, etc.: Paladin Books, Reprinted 1978), p. 74.
2. *Grimm's Fairy Tales*. Illustrated (New York: Airmont Publishing Company, Inc., 1968), p. 182.
3. Ibid., p. 180.
4. On pre-Shakespearean versions of the Lear story cf. Wilfrid Perrett: *The Story of King Lear from Geoffrey of Monmouth to Shakespeare. Palaestra XXXV* (Berlin: Mayer & Müller, 1904). Among Shakespeare's 'sources' there was also the Old Play, i.e. an earlier dramatic version of the Lear (Leir) story, cf. ibid., pp. 94 ff.
5. Geoffrey of Monmouth: *History of the Kings of Britain*. Translated by Sebastian Evans, etc. (London: Dent, Revised edition 1963), p. 35.
6. Cf. ibid., pp. 38-39.
7. Cf. Wilfrid Perrett, *op. cit.*, pp. 64-70.
8. Ibid., p. 75.
9. The *exemplum* is translated from a reprint ('King Lear at Tuebingen') in *Philologica: The Malone Anniversary Studies*, edited by Thomas A. Kirby and Henry Bosley Woolf (Baltimore: The Johns Hopkins Press, 1949), p. 227: 'APPENDIX II. Promptuarium Exemplorum Discipuli. Secundum ordinem alphabeti. Moguntiae M. D. C. XII. Exemplum XXXIX (Litera M), p. 421' (my translation).
10. Edward Bond: *Lear* (London: Eyre Methuen Ltd., Reprinted 1975), p.viii.
11. Jan Kott: *Shakespeare Our Contemporary* (London: Methuen, Reprinted 1965), p. 105.
12. William Frost: 'Shakespeare's Rituals and the Opening of King Lear', *The Hudson Review*, Vol. 10 (1958), p. 578 (my italics).
13. Cf. Jürgen Habermas: *Strukturwandel der Öffentlichkeit. Untersuchungen zu einer Kategorie der bürgerlichen Gesellschaft* (Neuwied und Berlin: Luchterhand, 5. Auflage, 1971), pp. 20-21 (my translation).
14. Umberto Eco: *The Limits of Interpretation* (Bloomington and Indianapolis: Indiana University Press, 1990), p. 24.
15. Michel Foucault: *Madness and Civilization. A History of Insanity in the Age of Reason* (New York: Pantheon Books, Random, 1965), pp. 18-19.
16. Ibid., p. 18 (my italics).
17. On Gloucester as a representative of superstitious credulity cf. William R. Elton: *King Lear and the Gods* (San Marino, California: The Huntingdon Library, 1966), p. 148: 'The old earl's mysterious universe of fear-inspiring eclipses operating at the behest of blind forces, offering omens of worse to come, was far from the ideals of Epicurean ataraxy. Like Epicurus, Plutarch pictured the superstitious man as a victim of ominous dreams, apparitions, ghosts, horrible shapes, voices, visions of bottomless pits full of torture and miseries.'

18. Jan Kott, *op. cit.*, p. 104.
19. Ibid., p. 104.
20. On theories of the grotesque cf. Wolfgang Kayser: *The Grotesque in Art and Literature* (New York and Toronto: McGraw-Hill Book Company, 1966). On Arcimboldo and his deconstruction of the classical unity of pictorial composition as well as his anthropomorphic landscapes cf. Gustav René Hocke: *Die Welt als Labyrinth. Manier und Manie in der europäischen Kunst* (Hamburg: Rowohlt, 1957), pp. 158-59.
21. Cf. Kayser's reference to 'a world in which the realm of inanimate things is no longer separated from those of plants, animals, and human beings, and where the laws of statics, symmetry, and proportion are no longer valid' (*op. cit.*, p. 21).
22. Mikhail Bakhtin: *Rabelais and His World* (Cambridge, Mass., and London: The M.I.T. Press, 1968), pp. 317-18. Cf. also on carnivalism in Shakespeare's *King Lear*, Michael D. Bristol: *Carnival and Theatre. Plebeian Culture and the Structure of Authority in Renaissance England* (New York and London: Routledge, 1989), pp. 209-13.
23. 'The Debate Betweene Follie and Loue'. Translated out of French by Robert Greene, Maister of Artes. In: *The Life and Complete Works in Prose and Verse of Robert Greene, M.A.*, Vol. IV. Edited by Alexander B. Grosart. *The Huth Library*. Printed for Private Circulation Only (1881-83), p. 223.
24. Cf. Erwin Panofsky: *Studies in Iconology. Humanistic Themes in the Art of the Renaissance* (New York, etc.: Harper & Row, Publishers, 1972), p. 105.
25. There are too many *ciphers* to decipher, and we may recall Walter Benjamin's problematization of allegorical *Zerstückelung* in his *Ursprung des deutschen Trauerspiels* (Frankfurt am Main: Suhrkamp, 1969), p. 206, where he refers to 'die Wollust, mit welcher die Bedeutung als finsterer Sultan im Harem der Dinge herrscht'!
26. Quoted from *Der Bilderkreis zum Wälschen Gaste des Thomasin von Zerclaere*, ed. by A. von Oechelhauser (Heidelberg: G. Koester, 1890), p. 25, n. 19, referring to a representation of *Diu Minne* (the God of Love) with the motto: *Ich bin blint und mach blinten.*
27. George Puttenham: *The Arte of English Poesie* (Cambridge: At the University Press, 1936), p. 191.
28. Cf. Harry Levin: *Christopher Marlowe: The Overreacher* (London: Faber & Faber Limited, 1965), p. 31.
29. This is how Lyly's style is characterized by Robert Ashley and Edwin M. Moseley in their introduction to *Elizabethan Fiction* (New York, etc.: Holt, Rinehart and Winston, Seventh Printing, 1965), p. xii.
30. *The Defence of Contraries* (1593) (Amsterdam and New York: Da Capo Press, 1969), facsimile edition of the text, title-page.
31. Stephen Prince: *The Warrior's Camera. The Cinema of Akira Kurosawa* (Princeton, New Jersey: Princeton University Press, 1991), p. 284.
32. According to Prince, with *Dreams* 'Kurosawa has returned to the dream-world and the imperatives of fantasy' (p 290). Cf. also his most recent film, i.e. *Hachigatsu-no-Kyoshikyoku* (*Rhapsody in August*, 1990), with its pessimistic emphasis on the insuperability of the past (= the bomb dropped on Nagasaki). Instead of making period films Kurosawa seems at present rather to focus on the surreal and apocalyptic quality of contemporary reality – a trend he already pursued in *Dodeskaden* (1970).
33. Stephen Prince, *op. cit.*, p. 14. However, Prince also emphasizes the 'different social structural values, which firmly separate the two classes of film' (p. 15).
34. Alain Silver: *The Samurai Film* (Bromley, Kent: Columbus Books, Revised and Updated text, 1983), p. 52.

35. Ibid., p. 52.
36. Cf. Stephen Prince, *op. cit.*, pp. 143 ff.
37. Cf. ibid., p. 146.
38. Jan Kott, *op. cit.*, p. 32.
39. Cf. Alain Silver, *op. cit.*, p. 19.
40. Ibid., pp. 22 ff. In Ran Kurogane's obligations towards his master Jiro collide with his inclination or natural conscience (cf. Kaede's treacherous behaviour towards the Ichimonji clan).
41. According to D.T. Suzuki, the samurai 'could never be separated from the weapon which was the supreme symbol of his dignity and honor' (Silver, *op. cit.*, p. 30).
42. Georg Lukács: *The Historical Novel* (Harmondsworth: Penguin Books, Reprinted 1976), pp. 106-07.
43. Alain Silver, *op. cit.*, p. 24. Thus there are two codes available to the samurai: (1) the code of revenge or (2) the code of ritual suicide (*seppuku* or *hara-kiri*). Unlike other Japanese directors Kurosawa pays little attention to the code of ritual suicide (cf. Hidetora's abortive suicide attempt *after having lost his sword!*).
44. *Folk Legends of Japan*, by Richard M. Dorson (Rutland, Vermont, and Tokyo, Japan: Charles E. Tuttle Co., Publishers, Sixth Printing, 1971), pp. 133-34. Cf. also 'The Fox Wife' in: *Ancient Tales in Modern Japan*, Selected and Translated by Fanny Hagin Mayer (Bloomington, Indiana: Indiana University Press, 1984), pp. 31-32.
45. In medieval art the geese sometimes hang the fox, but according to Kenneth Varty, 'In the many medieval stories about him, Reynard is often threatened with hanging for his crimes, but he is never hanged' (*Reynard the Fox*, Leicester: Leicester University Press, 1967, p. 81).
46. Cf. Dave Kehr: 'Samurai Lear', *American Film* (September 1985), p. 25. It is interesting to notice that Kyoami's (Peter's) transsexual status is parallelled in *King Lear* in Lear's confusion about gender identity, e.g. when he refers to '*Gonerill* with a white beard' (i.e. Gloucester, F, IV.6.2343).
47. Alan W. Watts: *The Way of Zen* (Harmondsworth: Penguin Books, Reprinted 1980), p. 137.
48. Dave Kehr, *op. cit.*, p. 24.
49. Stephen Prince, *op. cit.*, p. 147. Kurosawa makes this statement in the so-called Sato interview, cf. Roger Manvell: *Shakespeare and the Film* (New York: Praeger, 1971), p. 104.
50. Stephen Prince, *op. cit.*, p. 290.
51. Jan Kott: *The Bottom Translation. Marlowe and Shakespeare and the Carnival Tradition.* Translated by Daniela Miedzyrzecka and Lillian Vallee (Evanston, Illinois: Northwestern University Press 1987), '*Ran,* or The End of the World', p. 144.
52. Ibid., p. 145.
53. Ibid., p. 145.
54. Ibid., p. 148.
55. Cf. Hugo Friedrich: *Die Struktur der modernen Lyrik. Von Baudelaire bis zur Gegenwart* (Hamburg: Rowohlt, 1964), p. 24 ('leere Transzendenz') and p. 33 ('leere Idealität') and *passim.*
56. Jan Kott, *op. cit.*, p. 150.

The Face of Honour.
On Kenneth Branagh's Screen Adaptation of *Henry V*

Susanne Fabricius

Most of Shakespeare's plays make use of the past as subject matter and playground. Not only the dramas that we call historical, but also the tragedies turn times past into an arena for feelings and thoughts that could appeal to a renaissance audience. In Shakespeare the centre of focus is not on the historical, documentary reality, but on the emotions and moods of fiction. Just as he used men and women of the past for a present purpose, his plays are open to other and more modern interpretations.

Several of the tragedies use material which goes back to antiquity, while the historical plays are based on sources from the Middle Ages. Any Shakespeare production is like a jointed telescope – the Middle Ages seen through renaissance eyes regarded from the point of view of a current present. The telescope can be folded up and put back into the drawer to be taken out later and provided with a new joint.

Miniature and Close-up: Olivier and Branagh

What you see through the lens is neither the Middle Ages, the Renaissance nor the present, but the interpretation of universal forces in each period, struggling outside and inside man. In 1944 Laurence Olivier could utilise *Henry V* for a concrete historical and political purpose, the mobilisation of a patriotic fighting spirit at the end of World War II. Kenneth Branagh's version from 1989 could equally be seen as a reaction to the upheavals in Eastern Europe or to the debate on the English attitude to the EEC. But the new version could also be regarded as a wish to renew a stage succes. The 1984 stage production was considered the 'post-Falklands'-*Henry V*.[1]

But to relate the making of the film to specific historical events would lead to pedantic absurdities, as would a lengthy account of the social and economic conditions in England in the 15th century and during the Renaissance. The political and psychological themes in Shakespeare's historical plays are so universal and the wisdom and beauty with which they are handled so poignant and so realistic that they will reflect the latent or manifest conflict of any period.

Branagh has been anxious to make his film a contrast to Olivier's work. Throughout his introduction to the published version of the script[2] he refers to his predecessor who, in Branagh's view, while making the play popular, through his simplification of the text also created an obstacle to new productions. When The Royal Shakespeare Company produced the play, with Branagh in the lead and directed by Adrian Noble, it was the first stage production in 10 years.

Branagh pulls out his telescope, looks at the play through Olivier's film – in the negative – and then adjusts it. The effect is astonishing, for they appear as two totally different and completely independant *œuvres*. Olivier is hard to ignore and perhaps it is no coincidence that screen adaptions of Shakespeare's plays, after a pause in the seventies and eighties, were only taken up again after his death in 1989. Branagh's introduction, his choice of *Henry V* and the intentions behind his realisation can be considered a reflection of its young author's attempt to come to terms with the inheritance of the great father figure.

Olivier's film is a comedy, fit to inspire the English population with optimism and fighting spirit. According to his own statement Branagh tried to sell his project to the investors as 'a political thriller, as a detailed analysis of leadership and a complex debate about war.[3] Whether he has fulfilled these intentions is a matter of opinion, but the result is a film that does the text more justice than Olivier's even though it does not include as many of its words.

Olivier omits the scene of treason and Henry's threats against Harfleur – incompatible with his patriotic purpose as they are – but includes the leek scene between Pistol and Fluellen which Branagh has omitted. Where Olivier has pulled the teeth of the text, Branagh has subdued its conviviality. The poor, mad French king, Karl VI, is in Olivier's film depicted as a babbling contented child, in Branagh's as a – in an almost clinical sense – depressed man who cannot bear the power imposed upon him.

This fundamental difference in the mood of the two films manifests itself with visual distinctness. While Olivier's version all the way through is very bright, almost pastel, inspired by medieval miniatures, Branagh's is very dark. While the costumes in Olivier's film have colourful elements in the fashion of the Renaissance, they have medieval earth colours in Branagh's version.

The very use of the past implies both a distance to as well as a universalisation of the themes. The characters are at the same time drawn very close to

Charles VI (Paul Scofield) and the Dauphin (Michael Maloney).

and pushed very far away from the spectator, as when turning a telescope one way or the other. One moment they are quite close to us and invite identification, the next they are puppets in a play they do not control – a play which is either about fulfilling claims and expectations laid down by a set of rules, a law of succession, hereditary power struggles, intrigues; or about forces of the protagonists' minds of which they themselves are ignorant or do not control. Dynasties and their quarrels are magnifications of ordinary family conflicts at the same time as the characters' individual sizes are reduced, sometimes to the point of vanishing.

Shakespeare and the cinematic art are as made for each other. Both have the same telescopic quality – the ability to change between nearness and distance. *Henry V* has – with its battle scenes that in the theatre are left to the imagination of the audience – the viability of absorbing pictures and action. But the great drama is enacted in the mind. By virtue of its close-ups the film in this respect holds possibilities that no stage can offer. The moving picture is *the* medium of both the drama of the face and the clamour of the battlefield.

A Kingdom for a Screen

In the interaction between nearness and distance there is an irony that keeps total identification at arm's length. This is past, history, theatre, film – not reality. This is more than real.

Many of Shakespeare's plays have a meta-aspect apart from the ironic distance. A more sophisticated posterity has not needed to add that. *Henry V* has a frame, a chorus. In the film it takes the shape of Derek Jacoby. 'A kingdom for a stage, princes to act and monarchs to behold the swelling scene' he proclaims 'prologue-like' and points to the drama as a fiction – and that in spite of its dealings with 'real' things, and history itself. Is the stage an arena of history or history, the battlefield, an arena of fictions? asks the chorus indirectly, a question that has been asked a thousand times since then, and that you can ask yourself incessantly at any time. But how much better a true artist can create interesting characters and write stirring speeches than mediocre, opportunist politicians.

In neutral modern attire – grey coat and scarf – Jacoby contributes to a discreet topicality of the play, as does the film studio in which he strolls around. Within this frame Peter S. Donaldson finds a cinematic experiment, an effect of alienation, equal to those of Jean Luc Godard.[4] If this is so the experiment originates from Shakespeare and is precisely limited to the frame.

Branagh lets the play speak for itself. He uses a general contemporary cinematic language that lets the dialogue, the monologues and the actors shine. The text is of course drastically abbreviated, scenes and characters cut and the comments of the chorus moved around. On the other hand scenes are added – in flashbacks – originally from *Henry IV* and centered around the excesses in Henry's youth and the Falstaff character, his fatherly drinking companion.

Henry V is located in the middle of the chain of historical plays which taken together form a long and continuous story, though they are not written chronologically. *Richard II* was murdered by *Henry IV*, father of *Henry V*, himself father of *Henry VI* – here indeed is the forerunner of many a modern, endless television family saga.

Across the Threshold: To Be a Number in a Succession

After the prologue the chorus throws open the gate that separates the film studio from the film, the present from the past, reality from fiction. He does it with a vehemence that is contrasted both by his appeal to the audience: 'Your humble patience pray,/ Gently to hear, kindly to judge, our play' as well as by the insidious way in which the two warmongers, the Archbishop of Canterbury and the Bishop of Ely, open the door ajar in the next cut where they are plotting, ostensibly to pursue the lawful claims of the English throne, but in fact to strengthen the possessions of the church.

In the following scene, where the young king is introduced, an enormous double door is opened in a way that suggests neither vehemence nor ulterior motives, but which is dignified, majestic. The doorway frames the king's slight figure in silhouette against the light in the antechamber he is leaving, an image that has its parallel in the scene from the siege of Harfleur where the king is seen on his rearing horse in silhouette against a flaming breach in the ring-wall.

In the scene where he deals with the traitors, the king enters with soldierly bluntness. These entrances and openings of doors, which are one of the re-peated pictorial elements in the film, are not merely impressive visual effects, but also full of significance. It is most evident in the first entrance of the king where he grows before our eyes as he approaches the camera – all the time lit from behind. He crosses the threshold between youth and manhood, moves from the light into the darkness, into a world of gravity, decisions and tests of manhood, of power, deceit and war. We see the faces of the courtiers before we see Henry's. They see his face before we do.

In that scene Henry makes the big and to him unfamiliar decision of going to war. He hesitates when the clergymen appeal to him about the inherited ter-ritorial claims of the English throne. Only the French herald with the gift from the Dauphin – a set of tennis balls – succeeds in raising the fighting spirit in Henry's reluctant decision. The present is an insult to Henry's youth and (for-mer) wantoness from a person who himself – as it appears later on – has trouble growing up and obtaining the respect of his associates. Paradoxically the French herald, Montjoy, is the first to recognize Henry's capacities.

The three scenes open the film. They closely follow the structure of the play: the prologue, the scene between the clerics and the one in the council chamber are so perfectly linked and each so firmly and yet sensitively executed that they should become film history as one of the most consistent preludes ever. Words, meaning, acting and image form a completely coherent, organic whole, as if they had the same author. An author who – as does Branagh – identifies with the protagonist, the young king, who is finding his fixed place in the transition from a young man to an adult. The strong unity that the film is able to establish between itself and the text makes it impossible to keep them apart in the analysis – an analysis which, in this case, however, is marked by a pos-sibly uncritical enthusiasm for both film and text, an enthusiasm unspoiled by what others have called 'Branagh's studious and systematic campaign of self-publicity', since this campaign has not reached Denmark.[5]

Henry's vulnerability to reminders of his excesses combines with the in-herited adult responsibility that is imposed upon him. His hesitation to enter the war is linked by the play with his originally social and cheerful disposition as it was displayed in the bacchanals of his youth with Pistol, Nym, Bardolph and Falstaff. In the scene between Falstaff and Henry where they are seen as reverse reflections of each other, their faces betray violent changes of expression, from deep friendliness to freezing coldness in Henry and hurt astonishment in Falstaff. The scene ends off screen with these words that begin Henry's last line in *Henry IV*, II: 'I know thee not, old man.'

Like so many father figures Falstaff is also a bogeyman, an image of what could happen to Henry himself, a social superior who has come down in the world. His death in the beginning of the play is one of the preconditions for Henry's maturing into a grown man, a king. As a replacement for him enters the likewise bearlike, but upright and dull 'uncle Exeter', who has an appropriately submissive attitude to his sovereign.

But the complete film/play questions the value of his maturing. If Henry is a traitor to the friends of his youth, he himself is subject to the treason of others, as becomes evident in the following scene with Scroop, Cambridge and Grey who have sold him to the enemy. Henry plays cat-and-mouse with them. He has learned the grown-up-game – learned not to trust anyone, that cunning and deceit are part of life.

The topers of his youth – primitive as they are – know nothing of treason or hypocrisy. They mean what they say, and so they are young and unspoiled in mind though they are old, debauched and thievish. The deceitful, noble trio are interpreted by young, strikingly handsome actors, but they are full of double-dealings, and their tongues are false. In spite of their youth they are representatives of the (adult) world where Henry is now to hold a central place. He overcomes all internal and external obstacles and wins the French campaign after the siege of Harfleur and the battle of Agincourt, the latter contrary to expectation because the English army at that time is starved and decimated. As part of his spoils of war Henry receives the French princess Katharine in marriage. He has passed one crucial manhood test and is now ready for the next.

That's all! In spite of the fact that *Henry V* is very rarely produced for the stage, it is – along with *Richard III* – the only one of the historical plays that is generally known, thanks of course to Olivier's films. If Shakespeare has given life to the cinema, the cimema has indeed given life to Shakespeare.

Olivier's *Henry V* was meant to mobilise the nation and passed lightly over the fact that England is the aggressor in the play, and that the 'real' enemy was not France. Branagh's *Henry V* is, if not a pacifist work, extremely sceptical of violence. What makes the film interesting is its strong emphasis on Henry's conflict between the pressure to lay claim to the French duchies that he is subjected to and his 'natural' inclination to peace and his distrust of violence. The fact that the territorial claims are not only invented by his counsellors, but also by that part of himself which was raised to regard succession as a natural and important thing amplifies the conflict and makes it even more interesting. This conflict is not only a about a contradiction between the public and the private man, but also about a discrepancy *in* the private man.[6]

The Field of Honour

The dubious justification of war and violence is another main theme. It is developed on all levels, that of the monarch and his counsellors, of the officers and the men. Military and social precedence follow each other closely. At the bottom of both we find Pistol, Bardolph and Nym, the king's former companions from whom he had to distance himself when he ascended the throne. Nevertheless, they have to fight for his cause. The night before the battle Henry sets out, disguised in a borrowed cloak, to test the sentiments of his men. His ideal conception of an army is an equal, unanimous community, a brotherhood. But some of the men find it difficult to perceive that the honour of the throne is their concern, and Henry must come to terms with his growing isolation.

The question whether any idea is so important that it is worth the sacrifice of blood pervades the entire film. Because of the fact that the idea is something as flimsy as that of succession, it is ultimatively a question of honour – the pure idea or rather a pure emotional condition. And so the dilemma is pushed to extremes – physical life versus pure psychology. In the western world honour both at a personal and a national level ultimately means very little. It is not an advantageous position in which to understand our adversaries with another cultural background. *Henry V* is an early European example of the decline of the sense of honour and the rise of scepticism. Henry is to the same degree possessed with pride in his lineage and with democratic, humanistic and pacifist ideas.

The strong emphasis on Henry's pacifist inclinations is fully supported by the text, although the film evades the fact that in the text Henry orders the killing of the French prisoners of war. In that light his subsequent anger at the French killing of the luggage boys seems less justified. The play is just as full of contradictions as its protagonist.

Although it comes up with most of the arguments one can find against war, its climaxes are the peptalks the young king gives to the soldiers, 'Once more unto the breach' and particularly the famous St. Crispin's Day Speech before the battle of Agincourt, where all the odds are against them. They will lose their lives, but gain a name. The more superior the force one is up against, the greater the honour. 'We few, we happy few, we band of brothers.' The rhetoric of the play contrasts with its action.

As a spectator you have to acknowledge that you are subject to exactly the same ambivalence as Shakespeare and his young hero. No one could drag me into war, but sitting in the safe darkness of the cinema listening to Shakespeare's words out of Branagh's mouth my heart swells with pride and joy on behalf of both of them. Branagh is one of the happy few who can say everything in a single expression and a single tone. Just his face – in extreme close-up – and voice at the enunciation of this simple line in the beginning of the

We few, we happy few...

film: 'May I with right and conscience make this claim?' straight away give the extent of his disintegration, as does the contrast between his posture uttering the dreadful threats against Harfleur and the relief when the city surrenders. The examples are legion.

Mercy or Justice

The same conflict appears in the clash between his royal parentage and his youthful urge to carouse with the lower elements of the people, although the honourable turmoil of war has quite a lot in common with the harmless, but not as socially acceptable display of instincts of the bacchanal.

As Henry is in the dreadful predicament of passing final sentence on his former friend, Bardolph, for robbing a church, he delivers his judgement as a king – no indulgence to his friends – but he does it from a humanitarian motive: 'For when lenity and cruelty play for a kingdom, the gentler gamester is the soonest winner' (III.6.112-13). Clemency towards the enemy is more important than indulgence towards your own people. The film affirms the king's sanction of Bardolph's death penalty in a small silent scene that is added to the text. In the midst of the turmoil of the battle of Agincourt, Nym tries to rob a defeated French soldier, but is stabbed from behind. Death seems to be the logical consequence of greed. In spite of that, neither the play nor the film condemns the two thieves. Their shady morals are written all over them, but they are at least dishonest in an honest way and are aware of no sin.

But Henry is. Not only has he inherited a kingdom, but also a guilt to atone: his father Henry IV's murder of Richard II. During his restless stroll the night before the battle, in the 'Upon the King' soliloquy he pleads with God not to avenge this murder, which he has already endeavoured to expiate through an ample indulgence. Another of Henry's ancestors, the bloodthirsty Edward, the Black Prince, casts a shadow over his name in France. To Henry it is absolutely crucial to appear – to himself, his subjects and to the defeated enemy – not only as a just man of honour, but also as a man of lenience and mercy.

Those are the chords – and a few more – that he touches in the wooing scene. The main subject of the play, the justification of violence and war, is a terrifying one, not least with the passion with which it is performed here. So Shakespeare with his sense of variation has placed two sweet reliefs at the most-needed passages, after the siege of Harfleur and the battle of Agincourt – Princess Katharine's English lesson and the scene of proposal. The play/film does not resolve those serious issues in words, but with scenes and pictures. There is more to life than honour, politics, death and war – there is pleasantry, joy, flirtation and – maybe – best of all, love.

Mud, Muscles and Blood

But in the world of masculinity and power of the play/film these two scenes are only parenthetical. After re-reading the play Branagh characterizes it as follows: 'To me, the play seemed darker, harsher and the language more bloody and and muscular than I remembered.'[7] On the stage he tried 'to realise the qualities of introspection, fear, doubt and anger which I believed the text indicated: an especially young Henry with a little of the Hamlet in him'.[8] It is much easier to realise these aspects of Henry on film, with its possibilities of close-ups, low level dialogue, voice over and flash backs, than on the stage. Branagh regards the play 'as being tremendously "filmic", with an exciting linear plot, short scenes, great stuctural variety and several different strains of narrative providing a rich mixture of low life sleaze, foreign sophistication, action, philosophy and humour. In all seriousness, I was convinced that I could make a truly popular film'.[9]

This film is in fact created by Olivier. With its weight on the psychological aspects and 'the bloody and muscular language' it is hard to see Branagh's film as one of wide popular appeal. It is in all the meanings of the word a dark film – often with a single luminous spot or section in the picture, not to illuminate, but to create contrast. The bloody and muscular also pervades the film language.

As mentioned before the film has no experimental aim, but its action scenes, the siege of Harfleur and the battle of Agincourt, are of great technical and pictorial brilliance. The actual battle scene (6 min.) is rythmic-musical in its horror and full of observations of details in the combat that illustrate the themes. In the most bestial phases of the battle the film breaks into slow motion. As has been pointed out, the scene could be inspired by one of the – hitherto – dirtiest sequences of film history, the battle scene in Orson Welles' *Chimes at Midnight* (1965).[10] The use of the camera as well as the incidents in front of it become part of the narrative and the portrayal of the characters. The sequence is not a mere registration of turmoil.

While the corresponding scene in Olivier's version, inspired by Sergei Eisenstein's *Alexander Nevskij* (1938) (another film which set out to mobilise public opinion) is a clean, chivalrous ballet, performed on a well-groomed sunlit field of grass, Branagh and his fellow players roll in mud and blood. The sky opens its floodgates over the exhausted army, both during the battle and the march to Calais. After a lull in the rain during the march, it begins again as an ironic answer to Henry's line: 'We are in God's hands, brother, not in theirs.' If Olivier's film is a cutification of the play, Branagh's is a brutification. The nickname of the film, *Dirty Harry*, has its reasons.[11]

'Dirty Harry': Branagh and Ian Holm (Fluellen).

But although God, the French and all reason are against them, the English win the battle. It could be accidental, but as nothing is accidental in Shakespeare, not even when he is bound by historical facts, the explanation is to be found in the young king's strong urge to win the day and prove himself a responsible sovereign and commander. This urge is so powerful that it overcomes his own fear and that of the soldiers. The film is just as much about overcoming fear as about winning a war. In spite of its pacifist message it has elements that could make it more mobilising than Olivier's film.

Sublimely furthering that aim, too, is Henry's triumphal progress across the battlefield. It brings together the sweetness of victory and the loathing of combat in one long take (4 min.) of Henry carrying the body of a boy past his own people, past the defeated enemy to a cart where he unloads the body – where the scene ends in a close-up. It is accompanied by a fine Non Nobis, composed for the occasion by Patrick Doyle. The leitmotif recurs, delicately varied, throughout the whole film as background music accompanying the rhythm of the blank verse.

Gods, Puppets or Humans

That 'detailed analysis of leadership and complex debate about war'[12] that Branagh promised before the making of the film may not strike you as particularly full or surprising in the completed film. The words of the text on the loneliness of crowned heads and the horrors of war are indeed lavish and moving, but they hardly contribute to any new understanding of leadership or war. That would be asking too much of an almost 400 year old play. But the noble grandeur and heroism of the historical drama make the history of our own times look like yesterday's crumpled newspaper.

What would the world know of the Wars of the Roses and The Hundred Years' War without Shakespeare's plays and the respective screen adaptations? Without the great fiction of the novel, the stage and the screen, the knowledge of history wouldn't reach further than universities and school rooms.

The play/film's description of the complex transformation of a young man from wanton drunkard to a responsible statesman, commander and spouse in Branagh's interpretation is in its psychological insight quite novel and ranges much further than the mere telling of history. Whether Shakespeare's play, Branagh's film or both are the model for Gus van Sant's *My Own Private Idaho* (1991), which takes place among lumpen proletarian male prostitutes in present day USA, they indicate that the themes and wordings still have a great psychological and aesthetic impact.

The fact that the 'real' Henry V was only 27 when he fought the battle of Agincourt, and died at 35, puts the whole process in a peculiarly intense human and tragic light. When the closing tableau – the young king in a decoratively symmetrical arrangement with his beautiful bride – freezes, Branagh adjusts the telescope so that everything once again becomes a comedy, a miniature, infinitely distant, puppetlike and divine. Meanwhile the telescope has drawn a very universal human condition quite close to us for contemplation or identification – for no other reason than that it still lives and moves.

That is indeed sufficient!

Notes

1. 'Kenneth Branagh: Henry V' in *Players on Shakespeare 2*, eds. Russell Jackson and Robert Smallwood (Cambridge: Cambridge University Press, 1988).
2. Kenneth Branagh, *Henry V by William Shakespeare. A Screen Adaptation* (London: Chatto & Windus, 1989), p. 9.
3. Branagh, *Henry V*, p. 10.
4. Peter S. Donaldson, 'Taking on Shakespeare: Kenneth Branagh's Henry V', *Shakespeare Quarterly*, 42, Spring 1991, p. 98.
5. Graham Holderness, *Shakespeare Recycled: The Making of Historical Drama* (London: Harvester, 1992), p. 202.
6. Branagh, *Henry V*, p. 9.
7. Branagh, *Henry V*, p. 10.
8. Branagh, *Henry V*, p. 2.
9. Samuel Crowl, *Shakespeare Observed* (Columbus: Ohio University Press, 1992), p. 169.
10. For a futher discussion of this conflict in the play see 'Either/Or. Responding to Henry V' in Norman Rabkin, *Shakespeare and the Problem of Meaning* (Chicago: The University of Chicago Press, 1981). For Kenneth Branagh's interpretation of the rôle see Kenneth Branagh, *Beginning* (London: Chatto and Windus, 1989).

The Play(s) within the Film: Tom Stoppard's *Rosencrantz & Guildenstern Are Dead*

William E. Sheidley

> For the 'content' of a medium is like the juicy piece of meat carried by the burglar to distract the watchdog of the mind. The effect of the medium is made strong and intense just because it is given another medium as 'content'. The content of a movie is a novel or a play or an opera. The effect of the movie form is not related to its program content.
> – Marshall McLuhan, *Understanding Media*[1]

In a special case of McLuhan's theory, the 1990 film *Rosencrantz & Guildenstern Are Dead*, written and directed by Tom Stoppard,[2] 'contains' his classic 1967 play. Although it won the Golden Lion at the Venice festival, the film met with mixed reviews when released to the public. Some commentators waxed enthusiastic about the juicy morsel of its content, that is the modern comedy of ideas that seeing the film caused them to recollect.[3] Others complained that Stoppard's attempt to film his play destroyed it, making it too serious, too heavy, too dull.[4] Both groups failed to heed McLuhan's warning about the piece of meat that distracts the watchdog of the mind, responding either with delight or disappointment to the film simply as a vehicle for the play they remembered. Stoppard's film, however, does not merely translate a work of theater into a work of cinema; rather, it embodies a meaningful interaction between its 'medium' and its 'content'. The product of this interaction differs radically from the play it contains. Nonetheless, despite McLuhan's dictum that 'the effect of the movie form is not related to its program content', the effect of Stoppard's film depends significantly upon the particular nature of the play, or plays, that it contains and with which it enters into dialogue.

For Stoppard's film in fact 'contains' not only his own play but also Shakespeare's *Hamlet*, a good deal more of which is present than in the play. Stoppard says the additions were needed 'to provide more continuity to the story'[5] – a recognition of pressure from the realistic and real-time-oriented film medium, which McLuhan terms 'the reel world' (*Understanding Media*,

99

p. 284), on a scenario originally conceived as a series of conversations on a mostly bare stage where *events* mainly come as arbitrary intrusions from 'somewhere else'. Stoppard also remarks that he may have been 'more nervous back in 1967 about the conjunction of these two very different languages' (interview, p. 8). Of course it is exactly the contrast between the dashing, archaic, and mysteriously purposeful speech and action of the Shakespearean characters and the puzzled, analytical, and paralyzed conversations of Rosencrantz and Guildenstern that structures and animates Stoppard's play. There, the opposition between these two languages and the modes of being they express is resolved or frozen into eternal paradox by the triumph of the theater and its special reality, bumptiously represented by the Player and his troupe of Tragedians.[6] In the film, a new layer is added to the generic palimpsest of Renaissance tragedy and post-absurdist comedy, that of the realistic, full-color historical cinema, and the resulting structural tension or clash of visions necessarily incorporates an opposition between theater and film. The inevitable consequence, despite Stoppard's fairly close adherence to the story-line of his play, is that the resolution of the film's final paradox privileges not the eternal present of the theater but the ongoing temporal flux of the cinema.

Both plays that Stoppard's film mainly contains, his own and *Hamlet*, themselves also explicitly contain other plays or fragments of plays, and each derives a major part of its meaning from exploiting their interactions. A look at how the process works in *Hamlet* and Stoppard's play may help to clarify how it works in the film.

The Dual Function of *Hamlet*'s Inner Texts

In *Hamlet*, as Harry Levin pointed out long ago,[7] the contrast between the modes of discourse and representation characteristic of the Player's speech about Pyrrhus and of the performance of *The Mousetrap* on the one hand and of the main action of *Hamlet* on the other establishes the containing play as more realistic, complex, and true to life. At the same time, the parallels and differences between the actions and emotions represented in the insets clarify what has happened or may soon transpire at Elsinore. Both the audience on stage – variously Hamlet, Claudius, Gertrude, Polonius, and others – and the real audience in the theater see Shakespeare's characters reflected in these normative mirrors up to nature. A problem arises, however, from the inadequacy of the motivations and values portrayed in the archaic but comparatively intelligible worlds of the insets to compass the deceptive and complex world of the containing play. Thus Hamlet will soon hold his sword frozen above the defenseless head of his adversary, just as Pyrrhus does, but his ensuing action differs greatly from that of the Greek hero:

100

> ... after Pyrrhus' pause
> A rousèd vengeance sets him new awork,
> And never did the Cyclops' hammers fall
> On Mars's armor, forged for proof eterne,
> With less remorse than Pyrrhus' bleeding sword
> Now falls on Priam. (II.2.498-503)

Hamlet, however, lives not in the world of ancient epic but in a universe where killing your enemy may be to do him an eternal favor and destroy yourself, and where it is seemingly impossible to wield a 'bleeding sword' with unquestioned honor. He apprehends his world in a decidedly unheroic language, especially by contrast with the swelling rhetoric used of Pyrrhus:

> Now might I do it pat, now 'a is a-praying,
> And now I'll do't. And so 'a goes to heaven,
> And so I am revenged. That would be scanned. (III.3.73-75)

In short, what Pyrrhus does and the discourse in which his world is realized will not work for Hamlet, whose situation is thereby assimilated to our own condition of unheroic uncertainty. We recognize Hamlet's difference from Pyrrhus, but by the same token we refrain from judging him by Pyrrhus's values.[8] Similarly, the stylized dumbshow that precedes *The Mousetrap*, the wooden rhymed protestations of the Player King and Player Queen, and the forthright skullduggery of Lucianus fail entirely to represent the smooth social bearing of the 'real' king and queen in Elsinore or the antic disposition of the 'real' nephew to the king, who lurks murderously about the palace. And *real* is how Claudius, Gertrude, and Hamlet strike us as they, no different from ourselves, become the audience to Hamlet's play. In the words of Maurice Charney, 'the Player's speech ... [and] *The Mousetrap* play make a strenuous demonstration of Hamlet's reality right in the midst of Shakespeare's play'.[9]

But of course Hamlet is *not* real, only a character in a play. Our awareness of this fact, when coupled with the assimilation of our own world to Hamlet's that results from the artificiality and limitations of the insets, can have disturbing implications. As A.R. Braunmuller suggests, the evident theatricality of inset dramas in Renaissance plays emphasizes by extension the 'theatricality, duplicity, insubstantiality' of the containing play, 'and – by further extension – that of the audience's own extra-theatrical existence, which might indeed be a theatre of the world or a theatre of God's judgements'.[10] It is to the script of divine Providence in the theater of God's judgments that Hamlet finally means to adhere, but of course we recognize that the real author of his fate is Shakespeare, whose vision at best rests on a faith we may not share.

If all three levels – those of the insets, the doings at Elsinore, and the real world of the audience – are theatrical, truth may as easily inhere, if anywhere, in the more stylized show as in the more realistic. As Charney puts it, 'The real world of Claudius's court is a fiction'; *The Mousetrap*, 'by contrast, tells the truth of a secret murder' (p. 68). Such a recognition, coupled with the hypothesis that the theater of God's judgments may well be a stage on which we aimlessly wait for a God(ot) who never comes, premises Stoppard's treatment of this theme in his play.

Stoppard's Play: *Hamlet* Inside Out

Just as with Shakespeare's insets, the enclosure of a large part of *Hamlet* in *Rosencrantz & Guildenstern Are Dead* establishes a juxtaposition in which the postures, purposes, and problems of the *Hamlet* characters appear alien, inapplicable, or incomprehensible when viewed from the perspective of the universe evoked by the containing action. As a result, a world in which time seems to be stopped but death to be bearing down with unendurable imminence nonetheless and in which 'ninety-two coins spun consecutively have come down heads ninety-two consecutive times'[11] strikes the audience as not less but more true to life than a world in which 'your father, whom you love, dies, you are his heir, you come back to find that hardly was the corpse cold before his young brother popped onto his throne and into his sheets, thereby offending both legal and natural practice' (p. 51). The dilemma of Rosencrantz and Guildenstern as they await a doom they do not understand and cannot avert[12] is much more like our own than the motives and responses of Hamlet and the others. 'Now why exactly are you behaving in this extraordinary manner?' Rosencrantz asks Hamlet, as played by Guildenstern, to which Guildenstern replies, 'I can't imagine!' (p. 51). We may laugh at Rosencrantz and Guildenstern's inability to recognize some of the basic causative premises of the Hamlet plot, but a moment's reflection will remind us that the assumptions about identity, causation, memory, and will underlying those premises have already been called into question. The dialogue between Stoppard's play and Shakespeare's ensures that our laughter will not preclude our identification with the confused protagonists. These talking, reasoning, suffering, living men, whom we see as distinct individuals at grips with a remarkable set of problems, are superimposed on their indistinguishable and paper-thin Shakespearean counterparts, whose activities in *Hamlet* (spying, toadying) are despicable and whose deaths are negligible but deserved. The effect of the contrast is to promote our sympathy for Rosencrantz and Guildenstern, especially as the long string of coins coming up heads builds toward what Guildenstern terms 'the pure emotion of fear' (p. 17). It is with some relief, then, that we recognize them as literary characters from a play we know. No wonder they remember so little about their own past: nothing much was written about it. The familiar world of *Hamlet*, despite its complexities, offers a comforting illusion to the audience because it resembles the domain of ordinary 'probability' now lost to Rosencrantz and Guildenstern, a domain that 'related the fortuitous and the ordained into a reassuring union which we recognized as nature' (p. 18).

In Stoppard's play, recognizable nature is embodied in the inset fragments of Shakespeare's play. We encounter familiar Elsinore, however, not along the Jutland road but on a stage, where the Tragedians are about to enact number thirty-eight from their repertoire. Suddenly a coin comes up tails (fictional time has started moving), and immediately Ophelia's 'doublet all unbraced' speech from *Hamlet* (II.1.77-100) is acted out mutely before us. For the reader of Stoppard's play, the stage direction quoting the Elizabethan English of Ophelia's report represents a drastic change in discourse style from the cool, informal, and concise language of the previous stage directions and dialogue: we are now in a play. Here are love and rhetoric; blood will follow. On stage, this transition is marked by a change in the tempo of action, partly anticipated by the flamboyancy of the Tragedians, from the measured, understated gestures and speech of Rosencrantz and Guildenstern flipping coins to the impassioned, melodramatic gestures of Hamlet and Ophelia miming their heartbreak. The contrast paradoxically stresses the greater familiarity of the archaic fictional world of *Hamlet* by comparison to the strange real world Rosencrantz and Guildenstern were formerly inhabiting.

Of course a stage is exactly the place one expects to find a play, and Rosencrantz and Guildenstern, who turn their backs on a play about to be performed for them by the Tragedians, are the only ones who seem not to realize that the highway of their life has led them into one. Although they manage to slip into Shakespearean blank verse when accosted by the King and Queen and charged to 'glean what afflicts' Hamlet, they puzzle over their instructions and discoveries like fragments of obscure texts from an ancient civilization, lacking a frame of reference to explain them. Their unfortunate role in the play they have entered will be to die without understanding anything.

Real death may be incomprehensible, but stage deaths, as the Tragedians' tour-de-force performances on the boat attest, are entirely credible. Afterwards, the actors stand up, brush themselves off, and take applause, which may reassure us until we recall that actors are 'the opposite of people' (p. 63). Moments after the Tragedians' delightful series of stage deaths, Stoppard dramatizes the harrowing real extinction of Rosencrantz and Guildenstern as their simple cessation of presence. The intolerable state of dark emptiness lasts only an instant, for 'Immediately the whole stage is lit up' (p. 126), and we return to the fictional world of *Hamlet* with a sigh of relief. Momentarily at sea in what seemed to be reality, we come home to where in fact we have been throughout – in a theater, watching a show we have paid to have put on to entertain us.

That fundamental fact about the real existence of Stoppard's play accounts at least in part for the importance, indeed the dominion, of the Player and the

Tragedians within it. Although in one sense they are characters *in Hamlet* and *Rosencrantz & Guildenstern Are Dead*, the actors also *perform* versions of those plays, performances that reveal or even seemingly predetermine the fate of the characters they enact, even as those characters look on, audience to the depiction of what has happened or will transpire in their lives.

Now that Stoppard has enclosed *Hamlet* in his own play, the play that was enclosed in *Hamlet*, which as we saw contained a kernel of truth about the play that contained it, challenges for control not only of *Hamlet* but also of *Rosencrantz & Guildenstern Are Dead*. At one point, what appears to be Gertrude walks on stage and Rosencrantz, trying somehow to come to grips with the mysterious powers that hold sway over his existence, '*marches up behind her, puts his hands over her eyes and says with a desperate frivolity* ... Guess Who?!' (p. 75). It is Rosencrantz who has guessed wrong, however, for it is not the queen at all he is holding but the Tragedian Alfred, dressed for his part in *The Mousetrap*. As the Player and the other costumed Tragedians now suddenly appear from the wings, Rosencrantz and Guildenstern are trapped and hemmed in, forced to watch the dress rehearsal of a play that turns out to be not *The Mousetrap* at all, but *Hamlet* itself, in which they see two spies, representations of themselves, die as they will die. As they watch, they engage with the Player in a critical discussion of the meaning and stage representation of death, but, without warning, the rehearsal becomes the performance and the action of *Hamlet* sweeps onward, carrying Rosencrantz and Guildenstern with it.

Shortly, when they awaken at sea, 'all in the same boat' (p. 114) with the Tragedians and Hamlet, Guildenstern recognizes the degree to which he has become swallowed up in the dramatic illusion of the play within: 'I've lost all capacity for disbelief' (p. 100). Being on this boat, which is the stage, is like the secure existence of being in a text, where all your decisions are decided. Guildenstern deludes himself that all is well: 'Other wheels are turning but they are not our concern. We can breathe. We can relax' (p. 116). This is the illusionary condition of ordinary life, in which we carry on by ignoring the wheels that are turning, bringing us to our destined end. Guildenstern earlier has told the Player, 'I'd prefer art to mirror life, if it's all the same to you' (p. 81), and so, despite the Player's pregnant reply that to him, it *is* all the same, Stoppard's play does mirror life, by holding up to it a set of mutually reflecting imitations whose receding images contain in their abyss a powerful representation of the truth that distinguishes life from art, the reality of death.

The Plays Transformed in Film

Stoppard's exploration of the question of death in his play depends upon the interactions and interpenetrations of the nested fictions of which it consists.

The same process, now complicated by the addition of a new layer or 'container', this time in an entirely new medium, still functions in the film. If Stoppard's play is *about* the theater and its relationship to life, his film, in parallel fashion, reveals much about the nature of cinema and its different relationship to the life it represents. According to Charney, Stoppard in his play shares with Shakespeare and Pirandello 'a distrust for naturalistic drama ... constantly breaking the illusion and playing with the audience's expectations' (pp. 32-33). In his film, Stoppard definitely continues to play with the audience's expectations, but despite a notable series of anachronisms produced by Rosencrantz, the dramatic illusion remains intact. The modernist dramatic style of Stoppard's play places a premium on stasis and speculative verbal discourse, sacrificing theatrical illusion for metatheatrical awareness. By contrast, the cinematic style of his film places a premium on motion and the realistic representation of nature and natural historical time. Surrounding and containing the artificial, stopped-time worlds of theatrical fiction and abstract reasoning that dominate the play, the cinematically validated Newtonian real-time universe becomes the impersonal hero of the film.

The new visual elements brought to bear on the play now contained in the film wrap it in a world to which many of the play's preoccupations are inappropriate and for which its theatrical modes of representation and understanding are inadequate. They are nonetheless revealing, however, just as the Player's speech and *The Mousetrap* are inadequate to the mysterious world of *Hamlet* but provide keys to it, or as Hamlet's manner of confronting his fate does not apply to Rosencrantz and Guildenstern's struggle with an even more inscrutable universe, but helps to define their condition for us. Chief among these new visual elements are the powerful settings filmed in what was Yugoslavia. In the opening sequence, for example, Rosencrantz and Guildenstern come into view on horseback, already moving, against a stark rock face: hardly the place of 'no visible character' called for in the opening stage direction of the play. There, Rosencrantz and Guildenstern are to be 'well dressed'; in the film they are rumpled, dirty from travel, and bundled against the cold.

It is significant of the forward pressure of time in the film that the first words spoken are 'Whoa, whoa' to the horse as Rosencrantz stops to pick up a coin he sees lying in the road. Despite close-ups of the coin, which thereby becomes interesting as an object in itself rather than as a hypothesis in probability theory, the audience is distracted during the initial coin-spinning with intercut views of horses, gloves, the mildly interested face of Rosencrantz, and Guildenstern's impassive but ever-tenser eyes peering over the muffler that hides the rest of his face – all more sensuously forceful phenomena than the purely intellectual curiosity that the coin keeps coming up heads.

A quick cut forward in time puts our heroes back on the road again, Rosencrantz still flipping the coin as he rides, as the motion of the journey resumes. Thus there has been an interval of stasis sufficient to recall the feeling of the play, but it quickly dissolves. This defeats the suspense that builds into fear in the opening segment of the play because we have gone back to what was established as normal in the pre-coin segment of the film: forward movement through space and time. In the play there *is* no pre-coin segment, so a sense of progress through the space-time continuum is only established with the arrival of the Tragedians or the subsequent plunge into the *Hamlet* plot.

Trying to understand why the coins keep coming up heads, Guildenstern at one point hypothesizes, 'we are now within un-, sub- or supernatural forces' (p. 17), a proposition that seems a good deal more plausible on the bare stage of the theater than it does when he voices it in the film, by a campfire in a winter woodland, with horses grazing in the background visible through a light fog. The picture is of nature as in *camping out, getting back to nature* – far from the strange, non-natural space-time of a literary work, where Rosencrantz and Guildenstern find themselves characters in a play. As they converse in the film, Rosencrantz is preparing his meal just off screen, eventually lifting into view an elaborate Big Mac, complete with decorative toothpick. It is the first of a sequence of sight-gags about the distant future that punctuate the film, as Rosencrantz nearly discovers the laws of gravity and momentum and invents the airplane and steam turbine, while Guildenstern, preoccupied with the philosophical conundrums of their situation, ignores or inadvertently destroys his work. Not just words but things and events enter the film's dialogue. When, in trying to interpret Hamlet's remark about being 'but mad north north-west', Rosencrantz suggests 'He's at the mercy of the elements', a sudden gust of wind slams the door of the room. A moment later, the statement 'There is no wind' evokes a breeze that spins the makeshift windmill Rosencrantz is holding. Thus the natural world repeatedly mocks the characters' efforts to control and understand it, just as it shoulders into the film and rules over the plays it contains. While in the play the two characters are dwarfed and baffled by the important business of the *Hamlet* story, in the film it is the physical universe and the ongoing progress of natural time that sweep them, like us, along uncomprehendingly to their deaths.

The superior reality of the containing cinema to the theatrical works it contains is proposed forcefully by the arrival of the Tragedians in the natural landscape of highway and forest. Disturbingly physical and realistic as men, the actors are primitive and stylized in their performances as they preview their repertoire with bewildering speed and panache. It is a mistake to share Guildenstern's disdain for them, however, for their power, as in the play, soon becomes evident. Rosencrantz, fascinated by the attractiveness of Alfred, is frightened off in a scary bathhouse scene by some of Alfred's menacingly muscular colleagues, and it is through the physical vitality of the Tragedians that the film seeks to suggest the superiority of their art.

Rosencrantz and Guildenstern, in an even more direct manner than in the play, enter the world of Elsinore by way of the Tragedians' performance.

When the coin comes up tails, the pair are standing on the small stage of the Tragedians, illuminated by torches. Ophelia, pursued by Hamlet, bursts through the curtains, and the surprisingly realistic, cinematic scene that ensues seems momentarily to be a performance by the Tragedians. As pages from the Tragedians' promptbooks blow across the vast, polished floor of the castle, Rosencrantz and Guildenstern, blinded by the curtains from the Tragedians' stage that have fallen on their heads, stumble into the fictional world of Elsinore, which looks, especially by contrast with the Tragedians' shows, as real and natural as the woods and roadside from which they have been transported.

While Stoppard's play contained parts of *Hamlet*, the film contains both Stoppard's play and Shakespeare's, placing them on a structural par. The realistic cinematic mode prevents Hamlet, Claudius, Ophelia, and the rest from seeming any less solid and three-dimensional than Rosencrantz and Guildenstern, even though they speak Elizabethan blank verse. In the film, their presence is less dependent than in the play on how they speak, since we see them in so much greater detail. Stoppard gives a forceful and fairly traditional reading of *Hamlet*, with some striking innovations that mostly serve to remind us of the world of nature and time: Hamlet interacting with a chicken, sending a huge chandelier crashing down with a slash of his sword (the law of gravity confirmed), or forging the fatal letter to the king of England while sand slides through an hourglass beside him. In a newly invented scene, Hamlet dines with his two college chums over too much wine and clambers up on the table to declaim a few lines from the Player's speech about Pyrrhus, finally launching drunkenly into his famous discourse on what a piece of work is a man. As he does so, Rosencrantz, always alert to practical physics, reaches out to steady his wine glass on the wobbly table.

Hamlet punctuates his speech with a loud belch, which serves together with the bored and skeptical response of his friends to undermine both the idealism and the disillusionment that vie in the passage and in Shakespeare's Hamlet's mind. Thus audience sympathy for one of the characters in all western literature with whom readers most frequently identify is blocked. When Hamlet then, in a pretense of good fellowship, grasps and holds his friends' hands so hard that they are in obvious and comical pain as they try to pry loose, he appears to the audience, as he does to Rosencrantz and Guildenstern, a drunken bully whose sadism is, because of his rank and power, impossible to resist. Stoppard portrays the *Hamlet* characters in general as a dangerous aristocracy, and Hamlet himself as strong but not heroic, in that he remains throughout beyond the reach of our sympathies, which stay with Rosencrantz and Guildenstern.

Further to prevent Shakespeare's play from crowding out his own and taking over the film, Stoppard repeatedly employs the technique of viewing its action through windows, gratings, and peepholes, or from behind doorways or arrases. In this way he achieves in film the quality of remoteness and of being framed that marks stage action for the theater audience. Accordingly, we witness the arrival of the Tragedians' wagon at Elsinore through a window in the game room that opens on the courtyard. Shortly, we look over the shoulder of Guildenstern as he observes through a cross-barred window Polonius, Gertrude, and Claudius discussing Hamlet's love for Ophelia, and then follows the action through a series of other openings as the characters walk off down a hallway. Thus, with our heroes, we see *theater* through windows that separate it from us, but the separation is not secure, for the castle has doors as well as windows, doors through which the action of *Hamlet* and the Tragedians is liable at any moment to burst, surrounding Rosencrantz and Guildenstern and carrying them away. The intricacy of the magnificent castle itself, with its many secret passageways and the surprising ways in which rooms adjoin, helps Stoppard make the most of this technique. Sliding aside a panel in the wall opens a peephole that confronts one at terrifyingly close range with the blank mask of a Tragedian who has apparently been looking in a mirror on the other side of the panel preparing his face for performance; careless eavesdropping dumps one through a trapdoor into a woodbox, whose cover Hamlet nonchalantly lifts to say goodnight. Obviously, such a castle requires careful study to be understood, no less than the play whose action carries on within it.

Stoppard builds on the device he used in his play of gradually enclosing *Hamlet* within *The Murder of Gonzago* as staged by the Tragedians. The scene just mentioned in which Rosencrantz and Guildenstern tumble down a chute into a woodbox illustrates the nesting of plays and insets within the film. What they were spying on, through gratings and crevices, was the scene in *Hamlet* where the Player recites the speech about Pyrrhus while Hamlet, Polonius, and others look on. Thus we observe Rosencrantz and Guildenstern viewing part of *Hamlet* while the *Hamlet* characters serve as audience to one of its insets. Pyrrhus heroically strikes, Hecuba laments, the Player rants and chokes up, Hamlet seems moved, Polonius is bored, and our heroes, baffled by a pulley attached to a trapdoor on which they are standing, get dumped into the *Hamlet* plot by the operation of the laws of nature – not, as seems to be implied in Stoppard's play, by their suspension. Each level rubs corrosively at its neighbor, the ancient woes of Troy trivialized by the Player's professional tears, Hamlet reproached for lack of passion by the emotions of the inset performance, the seriousness of Hamlet's case undermined by Rosencrantz and Guildenstern's slapstick entry, and their own efforts to get a grip on human affairs at Elsinore mocked by their inability to master the physical objects whose contingent power over human life is stressed at every moment by the film.

As in the play, the complex interaction among these levels comes more and more to be dominated by the Tragedians and their leader the Player, who can patronize Rosencrantz and Guildenstern because he knows his way around Elsinore, having 'been here before'. A performance of *The Mousetrap*, done in a primitive but athletic style, takes place before an audience of servants, who loudly appreciate the elaborate dumbshow enactment of the as yet unfinished business of the *Hamlet* plot: an ocean trip, the death of Ophelia, a graveyard scene, a duel, poisoned wine, and two corpses representing Rosencrantz and Guildenstern. Later, we see a rehearsal of the dumbshow to be presented in court. Here, the actors are in masks and perform in a stylized Japanese manner, in rhythm to the music that is playing. Theatrical representation has now moved to an opposite stylistic pole from cinematic naturalism as well as from the realistic enactment of the nunnery scene from *Hamlet* that bursts, as in Stoppard's play, from backstage into the rehearsal. Thus Hamlet's passion is twinned with the stylized gestures of the dumbshow, and at one moment the dumbshow actress reaches out to comfort the real one. Next, behind a smoke screen set up by the Player, the film cuts to a scene in which the masked dumbshow characters are watching a puppet play that dramatizes their affairs, this time the poisoning in the orchard – yet another, even more artificial, layer in the nest of representations within representations. A real tear, however, drips from the puppet-murderer's eye. A puppet-avenger comes up behind the puppet-usurper-king, but it is not the dumbshow king, as we might expect, who rises calling for lights, but Claudius himself. Somehow the real court of Elsinore has materialized here, as Stoppard zooms us back without warning through multiple layers of artifice until we see Rosencrantz and Guildenstern again, still mystified, attributing Claudius's exit to his taste in plays: 'It wasn't *that* bad'. During this segment of the film, the Tragedians have enacted almost the entire substance of *Hamlet*, and we recall that indeed we seem to have got into Elsinore in the first place through their performance: the play that we – and they – have been *in* is itself *in* their repertoire.

The curtain that falls over Elsinore and this section of the film is the arras through which Hamlet has just stabbed Polonius, while he and our heroes and our camera-eye lurked behind it. The screen goes black, and what is Act 3 of Stoppard's play begins, on board ship, with sea sounds. When the action of both plays contained in the film thus leaves dry land and goes to sea, the dominance of theatrical reality over the cinematically represented natural world gets a boost. In Stoppard's play the boat *is* the stage, and the stage is all we see; in this part of the film the same is true, unlike the previous sections, for we now never see the ocean or anything else that could not be on a stage. Even the rollicking chaos of the pirate attack as filmed – we never see any pirates either – closely and pointedly resembles the same events as previously portrayed for the servants at Elsinore on their makeshift kitchen stage. A sexy bowsprit that in the kitchen performance had been portrayed by Alfred now appears as a real – but less realistic – wood-carving that crashes through the wall and hovers seductively over the sleeping Rosencrantz. Formerly attracted to Alfred and the prospect of getting 'caught up in the action' of one of the Tragedians' less tasteful performances, Rosencrantz now sleepily reaches out to embrace the wooden statue in a blissful parody of the immersion of life in art that constitutes his reality. Stoppard thus bends his film back toward the mode of representation characteristic of his play in order to reassert the founding premise of the Rosencrantz and Guildenstern story: that they are, in fact, not people but characters in a scenario they did not write and do not understand.

That theme has no meaning, however, unless the audience recognizes its own condition as metaphorically equivalent. In the play, audience identification with Rosencrantz and Guildenstern is powerfully climaxed by the death scenes, not the elaborate stage deaths enacted by the Tragedians or suffered by the *Hamlet* characters, but the contrastively much more real deaths of Rosencrantz and Guildenstern when they pass from presence to absence as the spots illuminating their faces on the otherwise darkened stage one by one go out. In the film, Rosencrantz and Guildenstern never seem mere characters in a play, but people, photographed in moving pictures. Their deaths are pushed back into *Hamlet*, and made gruesome enough by shots of the ropes going taut as they hang, but Stoppard seems to be striving for a balance between our identification with them, so readily accomplished in the film medium, and the artistic distance that allows a contemplation of the meaning of their fate.

At the end of a performance of Stoppard's play, the audience applauds, gets up, and leaves the theater. Life goes on. At the end of the film, life goes on *in* the film, namely the life of the group of men who are the Tragedians. They pack up their gear, and their wagon rolls off through the real landscape that was so strongly present in the earlier stages of the film. But *does* life go on? Not for Rosencrantz and Guildenstern, except as characters in a play that the Tragedians may stage – if they can find an audience, for, as the Player claims, 'the single assumption which makes our existence viable [is] that somebody is *watching*'. And surely life does not go on for long for us here in the commonsense Newtonian universe, unless, Stoppard may be implying, Someone is watching the theater of life, or unless at least we can somehow get into a play, or a film, the way Rosencrantz and Guildenstern stumbled into *Hamlet*.

Stoppard's film demands more than a passive response from its viewers, who must keep track of its continuous allusions to and differences from Shakespeare's *Hamlet* and the stage version of *Rosencrantz & Guildenstern Are Dead*. Stoppard signals this challenge by including the series of anachronisms that establish a historical perspective on the action locked into the late twentieth century and by from time to time rendering Rosencrantz and Guildenstern's antics in the familiar style of slapstick movies like those of Laurel and Hardy, the Marx Brothers, or Monty Python. In this way not just Elizabethan or absurdist drama but the cinema itself becomes a subject. Stoppard's play is a meditation not only on death but on the theater; likewise, his film is best viewed not, as some reviewers tried to do, as a cinematic version of that play, but as a different meditation, this time on death and on a new medium, the cinema, as well as on the plays that it contains.

Notes

1. Marshall McLuhan, *Understanding Media: The Extensions of Man* (New York: McGraw-Hill, 1964), p. 18.
2. *Rosencrantz & Guildenstern Are Dead*, directed and written by Tom Stoppard, based on his play; director of photography, Peter Biziou; music composed by Stanley Myers; production designer, Vaughan Edwards; edited by Nicolas Gaster; produced by Michael Brandman and Emanuel Azenberg; executive producers, Louise Stephens and Thomas J. Rizzo. Gary Oldman as Rosencrantz; Tim Roth as Guildenstern; Richard Dreyfuss as The Player; Joanna Roth as Ophelia; Iain Glen as Hamlet; Donald Sumpter as Claudius; Joanna Miles as Gertrude; Ian Richardson as Polonius. A Cinecom Entertainment release. 1990. Running time: 118 minutes. Further page references are included in the text.
3. For example, Michael Wilmington, *Los Angeles Times*, Feb. 20, 1991, pp. F1-F9; P. Travers, *Rolling Stone*, Nov. 29, 1990, p. 121.
4. For example, Terrence Rafferty, *The New Yorker*, Feb. 25, 1991, pp. 88-89; Hal Hinson, *Washington Post*, Mar. 15, 1991, p. C7; Ray Monk, *Times Literary Supplement*, May 24, 1991, p. 19; Vincent Canby, *New York Times*, Feb. 8, 1991, p. C14.
5. Stated in an interview with Peter Brunette, 'Stoppard Finds the Right Man to Direct His Film', *Los Angeles Times*, Feb. 20, 1991, pp. F1, F8-F9.
6. Jill Levenson, in '"Hamlet" Andante / "Hamlet" Allegro: Tom Stoppard's Two Versions', *Shakespeare Survey*, 36 (1983), 21-28, describes 'Stoppard's play as several transparencies stacked on top of one another' (p. 23), where the wit lies in the juxtaposition of points on different layers – Shakespeare with Beckett or Wittgenstein. She does not believe that the dialectic thus established ever reaches a resolution in Stoppard, nor in *Hamlet*, 'the world's most famous text whose infinite complexities defeat intellectual synthesis' (p. 25). The thematic bearings of Stoppard's play are by no means obscure, however. 'What Stoppard does', as Anthony Jenkins says in *The Theatre of Tom Stoppard* (Cambridge: Cambridge Univ. Press, 1987), 'is to exploit the comic potential of Ros and Guil's situation in *Hamlet*, a confused paralysis most cogently expressed in modern terms by Estragon and Vladimir's circumstances in *Godot*, in order to arrive at a statement about death that is both serious and of universal application' (p. 37).
7. Harry Levin, *The Question of 'Hamlet'* (New York: Oxford Univ. Press, 1959), pp. 138-64, esp. p. 161.
8. See among many others Peter Mercer, *'Hamlet' and the Acting of Revenge* (Iowa City: Univ. of Iowa Press, 1987), pp. 187, 193; and Richard T. Brucher, 'Fantasies of Violence: *Hamlet* and *The Revenger's Tragedy*', *SEL*, 21 (1981), pp. 257-70, p. 265.
9. Maurice Charney, *Hamlet's Fictions* (New York and London: Routledge, 1988), p. 34.
10. A. R. Braunmuller, 'The Arts of the Dramatist', in *The Cambridge Companion to English Renaissance Drama*, ed. A. R. Braunmuller and Michael Hattaway (Cambridge: Cambridge Univ. Press, 1990), pp. 53-90, p. 86.

11. Tom Stoppard, *Rosencrantz & Guildenstern Are Dead* (New York: Grove, 1967), p. 18.

12. Jenkins (47-48) suggests that Rosencrantz and Guildenstern could have chosen to tell Hamlet about the letter, thus taking command of their fates by a conscious moral decision. They would thereby, however, have ceased to exist as characters in Shakespeare's play.

Mel's Melodramatic Melancholy: Zeffirelli's *Hamlet*

Michael Skovmand

'I never liked the approach to the character that has been governing the choices and decisions for decades, this kind of wimpy dreamer who is impotent, uncertain in everything sexually, politically, humanly. I never saw Hamlet in those terms. For me, Hamlet is the quintessence of the New Man of the Renaissance.'

And who exactly is that?

'He is the first great modern character ever conceived by a writer,' enthuses Zeffirelli. 'So full of life, full of vitality, zest.'

...

'Shakespeare was looking for popular success. He was talking to a wide world, people of all social conditions and education levels. We have come to this horrendous, *monstrous* division of popular success and artistic success. This is ridiculous. This has been invented by cultivated people who don't like too many people having access to what they consider their own privilege and patrimony.'

(Excerpts from interview with F. Zeffirelli, *Empire*, May 1991.)

Very few literate people possess the cultural machismo, or the innocence, that would enable them to approach Shakespeare's *Hamlet* without at least some frisson of anxiety stemming from their awareness of the looming mass of commentary already generated by centuries of research and scholarship. They would suffer, in Harold Bloom's memorable phrase, the anxiety of influence. Interestingly, and refreshingly, Zeffirelli appears to be one of that few. There is very little Bloomian anxiety in the Zeffirelli production of *Hamlet*.

On the face of it, the combination of the Italian director Franco Zeffirelli and Shakespeare's *Hamlet* seems an incongruous one. The unwieldy, gloomy study of Danish sexual politics seems far removed from Zeffirelli's other Shakespearean screen productions: the glamourous romp of the Burton/Taylor *Taming of the Shrew* from 1966, his *Romeo and Juliet* from 1968 which fed directly into the Zeitgeist of 'don't trust anyone over 30', and even his film version of Verdi's *Otello* fron 1986, a lush and spectacular production featuring Placido Domingo and Katia Ricciarelli.

In the following, I shall argue that the Zeffirelli *Hamlet*, whilst offensive to some scholarly traditions, makes interesting, albeit problematic sense. Crucially, the prism through which I read Zeffirelli is the term *melodrama*, more particularly with the inflection given to the term by Peter Brooks in his study from 1976, *The Melodramatic Imagination*.

Hamlet: History, Tragedy, Problem Play or Melodrama?

Hamlet has always been generically problematic. By origin it is a history play, with its narrative antecedents in Saxo and Belleforest, and is thus on a par with two other Shakespearean plays drawing on murky historical sources: *Macbeth* and *King Lear*.

Belleforest's *Hamlet* was translated into English in 1608 as *The Hystorie of Hamblet*. Shakespeare's play was registered in 1602 as *A booke called the Revenge of Hamlett Prince Denmark;* it was published in 1603 (first Quarto) as *The Tragicall Historie of Hamlet Prince of Denmarke*, and ultimately, in the 1623 Folio edition, it was entitled *The Tragedie of Hamlet, Prince of Denmarke*. The Folio collection operated with only three divisions: (a) histories, (b) comedies and (c) tragedies. These were rough and ready categories, indicating whether the narrative structure was dictated primarily by accounts of past events, was geared towards a happy/upbeat or unhappy/downbeat ending. The ambiguous history of the title of *Hamlet* reflects structural and thematic ambiguities of the play. It can be argued that it is not a history, since historical re-presentation, truthful or otherwise, is not a major concern of the play. Is it a tragedy? A moot point, the intricacies of which cannot be entered into in this essay. Suffice it to say that neither as a classical tragedy nor as a revenge variant is it entirely unproblematic. The notion of the 'flaw' of the protagonist is debatable, the catharsis of the ending equally so. The moral and narrative efficacy of the 'revenge' is dubious, to say the least.

The invention of the category 'problem play', while well suited to a play such as *Measure for Measure*, does not fit the sprawling and complex structure of *Hamlet*. The play, to use T.S. Eliot's famous phrase, is one of *excess*. In the context of his famous formulation of his poetics of the 'objective correlative', the *excess* emotion in *Hamlet* is seen as a major flaw in the play:

> The artistic 'inevitability' lies in [this] complete adequacy of the external to the emotion; and this is precisely what is deficient in *Hamlet*. Hamlet (the man) is dominated by an emotion which is inexpressible, because it is in *excess* of the facts as they appear. And the supposed identity of Hamlet with his author is genuine to this point: that Hamlet's bafflement at the absence of objective equivalent to his feelings is a prolongation of the bafflement of his creator in the face of his artistic problem.[1]

Eliot concludes his critique of *Hamlet* by stating quite baldly that 'We must simply admit that here Shakespeare tackled a problem which proved too much for him'.[2] I submit that this conclusion is more appropriately applied to Eliot himself: his bafflement in the face of *Hamlet* is a dramatization of the inadequacy of his 'objective' poetics. Eliot does not go so far as to say that *Hamlet* as a play is an experiential failure, from an audience point of view. What he is saying is that according to his poetics it ought to be. This in turn might have led Eliot to reconsider the adequacy of his conceptual 'tools' in dealing with *Hamlet*. Had Eliot lived longer, he might have found Peter Brooks' analysis of melodrama as 'the mode of excess' interesting. The term melodrama has traditionally been applied pejoratively to a range of popular literature, and Brooks' *The Melodramatic Imagination* (1976) is a deliberate attempt to rehabilitate the term as a descriptive critical category, and is in the process, an attempt at a revaluation of melodrama in general. Historically, Brooks locates the rise of melodrama as coinciding with the development of early Romantic drama, and with the rise of the novel. Brooks, unlike other critics such as Eric Bentley, Robert B. Heilman or James L. Smith, hesitates to use the term melodrama in its extended generic sense, although he recognizes the legitimacy of doing so (p.xi). Nevertheless, Brooks' general characterization of melodrama illuminates much of the generic confusion which gave rise to Eliot's 'bafflement', and which has persistently created a conceptual mystique in critical and productive approaches to *Hamlet*. Brooks' description of melodrama as the irruption of Modernity with the French Revolution is, *mutatis mutandis*, applicable to the Renaissance Modernity of *Hamlet*:

This is the epistemological moment which it illustrates and to which it contributes: the moment that symbolically, and really, marks the final liquidation of the traditional Sacred and its representative institutions (Church and Monarch), the shattering of the myth of Christendom, the dissolution of an organic and hierarchically cohesive society, and the invalidation of literary forms – tragedy, comedy of manners – that depended on such a society. Melodrama does not simply represent a 'fall' from tragedy, but a response to the loss of the tragic vision.[3]

In parallel with the idea of 'the liquidation of the Sacred', Brooks points to the 'expressionist' dimension of melodrama – he defines it as 'the expressionism of the moral imagination' (55). Interestingly, he points out how melodrama persists in focusing on *muteness* as an extreme version of the problematics of articulation:

One is tempted to speculate that the different kinds of drama have their corresponding sense deprivations: for tragedy, blindness, since tragedy is about insight and illumination; for comedy, deafness, since comedy is concerned with problems in communication, misunderstandings and their consequences; and for melodrama, muteness, since melodrama is about expression. (57)

Finally, Brooks couples melodrama and psychoanalysis, a nexus which makes historical sense, but which also accounts for the attractiveness of Oedipal readings of Hamlet's predicament:

> Psychoanalysis can be read as a systematic realization of the melodramatic aesthetic, applied to the structure and dynamics of the mind. Psychoanalysis is a version of melodrama first of all in its conception of the nature of conflict, which is stark and unremitting, possibly disabling, menacing to the ego, which must find ways to reduce or discharge it. The dynamics of repression and the return of the repressed figure the plot of melodrama. Enactment is necessarily excessive: the relation of symbol to symbolized (in hysteria, for instance) is not controllable or justifiable.[cf.Eliot's 'objective correlative' (MS)]. Psychoanalysis as the 'talking cure' further reveals its affinity with melodrama, the drama of articulation. (201-2)

Zeffirelli's Narrative Choices

Melodrama, historically and etymologically, is drama accompanied by music. The production and direction of opera, the dominant Italian version of melodrama, has been Zeffirelli's primary professional domain throughout his career, and consequently his Shakespearean films have routinely been tagged 'operatic'. In the following analysis of Zeffirelli's *Hamlet*, I shall attempt to demonstrate how the overall approach to the production is melodramatic, occasionally specifically operatic, and how this approach opens up a number of perspectives and shuts out others.

Although The Zeffirelli *Hamlet* cannot be said to represent a *radical* departure from Shakespeare's established text, the text editors, Zeffirelli himself and Christopher de Vore, have made a number of major deletions and transpositions which significantly shift the balance of the play.

The opening scene – a funeral ceremony for Old Hamlet in the vaults of Elsinore Castle, preceded by an establishing shot of the castle and a lengthy take with the camera travelling and zooming its way into the courtyard, past a multitude of immobile soldiers and into the vault itself – is a classic expository scene, firmly anchoring the narrative within the genre of the family melodrama. Indicative of this is the shot of Hamlet, Gertrude and Claudius, the central triangle, placed around the body of Old Hamlet, preceded by the very first diegetic sound of the film, the sound of a woman – Gertrude – sobbing. In many ways this expository device can be compared to the opening scene of Olivier's film *Richard III*, in which the coronation scene – taken from *Henry VI, Part 3* – is given this expository function. In both cases we see a significant triangular pattern of gazes, establishing a field of sympathies and conflicts, and raising our dramatic expectations. However, whereas in *Richard III* this addition makes narrative sense, in that it establishes the historical continuity

Publicity still, emphasizing the family melodrama.

of the Henriad, a task left in the play to Richard's 'Winter of Discontent' soliloquy, in Zeffirelli's *Hamlet* the opening scene in the vault replaces the entire Scene 1 of the play – an opening scene justly famous within the Shakespeare oeuvre for its haunting creation of an opening mood ('Tis bitter cold, and I am sick at heart') and its establishment of a situation of military alert and spiritual confusion, i.e. an establishment of a far wider range of signification than in the Zeffirelli opening scene. As Jonathan Romney points out, this deletion makes for a far less 'metaphysical' *Hamlet* than usual (5). Obviously, this is in part due to the deletion of the Fortinbras story in Zeffirelli's *Hamlet*, a deletion which has a whole range of consequences, among which are not only the elimination of that claustrophobic, almost siege-like mentality we get from Scene 1, but a general reduction of the social and political dimensions of the story. Furthermore, it robs us of the obvious point of comparison between Hamlet and Fortinbras, between the doubter and the doer. Admittedly the Fortinbras story, with all its ramifications (Voltemand, Cornelius, etc.) is an obvious candidate whenever a producer of *Hamlet* has to get down to the inevitable task of cutting. In the 1948 film Olivier, and Alan Dent, the editor, managed to cut out not only Fortinbras but Rosencrantz and Guildenstern (with Polonius taking over some of R and G's lines), leaving us with a *Hamlet* very much focused on the psychology of the protagonist (and giving a lot of screen time to Olivier himself). Zeffirelli, fortunately, kept Rosencrantz and Guildenstern, and the scenes in which they are involved with Hamlet are among the most successful in the film, bringing out as they do a Hamlet who is more interactive and resourceful, and thus better suited to both Gibson as an actor and to the overall concept.

The opening scene, then, is one of several examples of Zeffirelli's essentially *melodramatic* approach in concrete action: situations are, as it were, 'disambiguated' to create a superfluity – or *excess* – of simple signification, in which effects do not work in counterpoint, but in *amplification* of each other.

Another example of 'disambiguation' which, however, is more successful, is the bold shift of the 'nunnery' injunction from the 'nunnery scene' itself to the play within the play. Already Zeffirelli's shift of the 'To be or not to be' soliloquy from before to after the Nunnery scene (a frequent transposition, most famously in the 1949 Olivier *Hamlet*) implicitly interprets the soliloquy as being motivated by the frustrations stemming from Hamlet's exchange with Ophelia. Leaving the nunnery injunction ('Get thee to a nunnery...') out of the Nunnery scene and shifting it to the play within the play, gives it a more logical context, placing this rather definitive statement in what is effectively the last scene with Ophelia and Hamlet together, their only later 'encounter' being at Ophelia's funeral.

Crucially, the Chapel Scene (Act III, sc. 3), our only opportunity to get a sustained inside look at Claudius on his own, bears witness to this strategy of 'disambiguation'. Claudius, the antagonist of the play, must be painted sufficiently black to provide the motivation for Hamlet's quest for revenge. On the other hand, a traditional arch villain would make Gertrude's infatuation look unmotivated or perverse, and would make Hamlet's hesitation damning or unintelligible. In other words, Claudius needs to be a *complex* character. In the play, the Chapel Scene provides that complexity, the central dilemma being expressed like this:

> – 'Forgive me my foul murder?'
> That cannot be, since I am still possess'd
> Of those effects for which I did the murder –
> My Crown, mine own ambition, and my queen.
> May one be pardon'd and retain th'offence? (III.3. 52-56)

Claudius' 39 lines alone in the chapel, agonizing out this dilemma, are reduced in the film scene to these four:

> O, my offence is rank, it smells to heaven;
> It hath the primal eldest curse upon't –
> A brother's murder....
> O wretched state! O bosom black as death! (III.3. 36-8, 67)

The psychological *complexity* of the full speech is reduced to the *excessive* expressivity of melodrama, giving vent to a *simple* state of mind: 'O, O, O!'

Other major examples of melodramatic simplification occur in the excision of the first half of the soliloquy 'O what a rogue and peasant slave am I' (II.2. 544-601) – in the Zeffirelli version the soliloquy starts with the line 'Am I a coward?' (l.566). This excision is a consequence of the excision of practically all of the long scene in which Hamlet meets the players, except for Hamlet's dialogue with Polonius about 'using the players according to their desert' (II.2. 518-528), and the *total* elimination of Hamlet's instructions to the players (III.2. 1-45). This supports the interpretation of a far less *intellectual* Hamlet than ordinary. Add to this the deletion by Zeffirelli/de Vore of 'How all occasions do inform against me', a soliloquy which, though triggered by the chance meeting with Fortinbras, actually contains no direct reference to Fortinbras, which means that if required it can be used in a production in which Fortinbras is cut out.

By the same token, it makes excellent *melodramatic* sense to have the Nunnery Scene plus 'To be or not to be' shifted to before the introduction of the players and Hamlet's resolution to 'catch the conscience of the King'. This creates an unbroken continuity between the arrival of the players and the play within the play.

These transpositions and deletions create an unswerving dramatic trajectory of Hamlet's development, in which he makes his decisive move away from passivity and delay by staging the play. This move is followed up by the Closet scene with Gertrude, which is an acting out of the personal implications of turning to action: the killing of Polonius, and confronting his mother with the 'truth' about Claudius. Then comes the exuberance of at last facing up to

Claudius (Act IV, sc.3); and finally there is the hoisting of Rosencrantz and Guildenstern with their own petard. These are seen as the unambiguous consequences of Hamlet's personal development away from the wimp of the first two acts and into becoming a man of action. From this dramatic trajectory follows at least two things necessarily follow: one, the difficulty of making Act V anything but anticlimactic, or simply an epilogue, and two, an almost total elimination of the theme of madness. Zeffirelli attempts to counteract the potential anticlimax of Act V by stretching the conspiracy scenes between Laertes and Claudius into Act V, which in Shakespeare consisted only of two long scenes: the gravedigger scene, plus an interior scene which modulates uninterruptedly from Hamlet and Horatio alone through the entrance of Osric the courtier and on to the final fencing scene. The Osric intermezzo traditionally provides comic relief not only through its banter, but also through the overly affected/homosexual acting of the part of Osric. Not so in Zeffirelli. He probably found the conventional gay-bashing of the scene offensive, but more importantly, comedy at this point would appear disruptive, just as he was setting a sombre mood, with a pensive Hamlet looking at a heavily symbolic setting sun, right after the cross-cut from Claudius and Laertes plotting about the use of poison. Dramatically this is a simplification, but a defensible one, since Hamlet's goading of Osric is little more than a repeat of what he did earlier to Polonius; if kept in full, it might indicate that he had undergone little or no development since early in the play. This is not to say that sombreness reigns for the rest of the scene, and the play. In fact, Gibson/Zeffirelli manage to inject a good deal of hilarious but poignant horseplay into the fencing scene – a scene of grotesque overacting from Gertrude (Glenn Close) and Claudius (Alan Bates), but with predictable gusto and vigour from Gibson.

The idea of 'putting on an antic disposition' – an element inherited from Saxo, where it made sense as a strategy for survival, but in the Shakespearean context always a rather dubious ploy – is practically non-existent in Zeffirelli. This in turn makes it more difficult to build up an atmosphere of hypocrisy, of spying and counterspying, although Zeffirelli attempts to do so through a number of mise en scene moves not authorized by the Shakespearean text: Hamlet is seen to overhear Polonius' fatherly injunction to Ophelia to stay away from him, just as Polonius is made to eavesdrop on Hamlet's 'madness scene' with Ophelia (Act II, sc.1); Hamlet overhears Ophelia being 'loosed' on him before the nunnery scene, and Hamlet sees the conspiratorial meeting of Rosencrantz and Guildenstern with Claudius.

The 'disambiguation' approach coincides with, but is separate from, the necessary verbal pruning of a play as long and wordy as *Hamlet*, a process of condensation and visualization of which there are many strikingly creative examples in this film.

One is Hamlet's scene with Ophelia (Act II, sc.1). In the play this is reported to Polonius by Ophelia; in Zeffirelli it is acted without speech, but with

Horseplay at Elsinore.
Mel Gibson, Nathaniel Parker (Laertes) and John McEnery (Osric).

Polonius spying – a logical and economical solution. Ophelia's reported speech ('My Lord, as I was sewing in my closet/ Lord Hamlet, with his doublet all unbrac'd'... etc.) cries out for visualisation, and Polonius might as well see the scene for himself. This is a far better solution than that of the 1948 Olivier film, in which a silent vignette was accompanied by what was, from the audience's point of view, a redundant report by Ophelia. The other three major examples of reported, off-stage action – The Ghost telling of his murder, the undoing of Rosencrantz and Guildenstern, and the drowning of Ophelia (all of which were done by Olivier by means of visual vignettes in an iris framing, all of which were utterly undramatic since they simply added a visual equivalent of the voice-over) – all of these are done simply and effectively by Zeffirelli. He lets the ghost speak without visual aids, since the story is powerful enough on its own (and will in any case be reenacted in 'the play within the play'). He dramatizes the scene on board the ship directly, adding a shockingly effective clip of Rosencrantz and Guildenstern being dragged screaming to the block, and finishing off with the sickening sound of the axe (in the Tower, presumably). The drowning of Ophelia is a special case, however, in that Gertrude, who reports the incident to Laertes and Claudius, cannot have been an eyewitness (or she would at least have tried to save her!). Whereas in the play there are several events (the letter from Hamlet, the conspiring of Laertes and Claudius) occurring between Ophelia's second madness scene and her drowning, in Zeffirelli, through a number of jump dissolves, she runs directly from the castle to the brook, whereupon the voiceover of the queen accompanies a dissolve to the previous interior scene in the castle, with the queen simply *telling* the strikingly visual story of the drowning:

> There is a willow grows askant the brook
> That shows his hoary leaves in the glassy stream
> Therewith fantastic garlands did she make
> Of crow-flowers, nettles, daisies, and long purples... (IV.7. 165-68)

An effective and economical presentation of the scene, the crowning touch of which is the final cut to a high-angle shot of a barely recognisable human form in the river, the camera then rising beyond the surrounding hills, a jump dissolve making the connexion to two riders on horseback – Hamlet and Horatio, on their way to the gravedigger scene, making the theme of death an appropriate tie-in to the final act.

Zeffirelli's Use of Space

At the heart of Zeffirelli's use of space is his sense of Elsinore. Olivier, in 1948, saw Elsinore as a symbolic structure, a *mindscape* in which high and low planes, winding staircases, ever-receding portals, beds, chairs and crucifixes, all interwoven by a wandering, disembodied camera, functioned as symbolic, psychological signifiers, leaving us with very little sense of a concrete historical place called Elsinore. Kozintsev, in his recreation of Elsinore, gave us another kind of symbolic structure: a hyper-historical embodiment of oppression and corruption, in which the brute physicality of stone, fire and servitude became a representation of the ongoing class struggle from the perspective of historical materialism.

Zeffirelli's approach approach to Elsinore is essentially that of *picturesque naturalism*. That is to say, Zeffirelli represents a sanitized, Italianate version of the average imaginary conception of a Renaissance castle, complete with peasants, soldiers, courtiers and all the clutter of indoor 16th-century activities of scholarship, weaving, embroidery etc., but very little sense of the filth, the physical proximity of people and animals kept inside the castle, the lack of personal hygiene, etc. Pauline Kael's nasty comments on this stagy/operatic aspect of the Zeffirelli mise en scene in *Romeo and Juliet* may to some extent be applied to his *Hamlet*:

Theatricality can be effective in a movie when it is consciously used, but it's very awkward when the director is trying for realism – which Zeffirelli apparently takes horse-play and opulent clutter, and dust, to be. He brings to the screen the filler of opera – all that coarse earthy stuff that comes on when the main singers are off. And Zeffirelli's 'robust' realistic detail is ludicrous; when he throws a closeup of the marketplace onto the the screen and we see peppers and onions, it's like the obligatory setting of the scene in the first act of an opera when the peasant girl walks on with the basket on her arm.[7]

The cinematic strategy with which Zeffirelli approaches Act I, Sc.2, the court scene, is a good example of how he *narrates* with the spatial dimensions of the story in mind. Whereas Olivier in 1948, and Kozintsev in his 1964 Russian version, grasp the opportunity to foreground the public, representative nature of both Claudius' marriage to the widowed queen and the assumption of power by Claudius, Zeffirelli 'privatizes' the exchanges with Laertes and Hamlet, splitting up the scene into three: the royal proclamation in the great hall, Laertes' petition to go to France in the library (a location to be used later in the 'words, words, words' scene), and the interchange between Hamlet, Claudius and Gertrude in Hamlet's study – a dark, musty room cluttered with books and scientific paraphernalia. Furthermore, this last interchange is re-arranged in such a way that, instead of being organized around the triangular tension between Claudius, Hamlet and Gertrude, the King exits, leaving to Gertrude words which in his mouth are hypocritical ('This gentle and unforc'd accord of Hamlet/Sits smiling to my heart'), thus depriving the scene of much of its irony and ambiguity.

The ensuing soliloquy ('O that this too tooo sullied flesh...'), is in consequence less motivated than in the play, because it is not a reaction to Gertrude and Claudius *together*, but follows upon Hamlet's exchange with Gertrude alone.

All in all, the rearrangement of the court scene, while creating variety and dynamism in the mise en scene and avoiding the theatrical *blocking* of actors, engenders shifts of emphasis in character relations which appear to be neither consistent nor altogether intentional.

An exceedingly positive, indeed enthusiastic reading of Zeffirelli's use of space (and light) can be found in David Impastato's two articles 'Zeffirelli's *Hamlet* and the Baroque' and 'Sunlight Makes Meaning',[8] in which he identifies Zeffirelli's overall style as the seventeenth century 'Baroque' style of Rembrandt, Vermeer, Velasquez and Caravaggio, in contrast to the 'Mannerism' of Olivier's 1948 *Hamlet*:

... the art of the Baroque is open, fluid, emotionally expansive, sensuously free. A 'naturalism' returns to color, the human form and the physical environment. But above all, Baroque art is distinguished by its quality of light, which moves over and around forms and colors to create a sense of living presence, a nurturing dynamic of action as well as repose ... The result is no mere 'geo-historical authenticity but a poetic and allusive naturalism ...'[9]

Indeed, at its best, the Zeffirelli *Hamlet* moves beyond touristy Technicolour and achieves exactly that – a 'baroque' richness, where the physical details of the setting are transformed from 'clutter' to 'poetic naturalism'. Two striking instances of this are the 'To be or not to be' soliloquy in the crypt, and the outdoor tavern scene with Rosencrantz and Guildenstern, carrying over into the introduction of the players.

The choice of the cavernous crypt, complete with skulls, bones, sarcophaguses and the odd dusty sunbeam for the 'To be or not to be' soliloquy is a happy, if obvious, one. The location is already established in the minds of the audience as the funeral parlour of the opening scene. The place reeks of death, more specifically Old Hamlet's death. There is less need for the theatricality of, for example, a declamatory Laurence Olivier perched on the topmost platform of a tower; the place, as it were, speaks for itself.

The scene from Act II between Rosencrantz, Guildenstern and Hamlet, placed as it is in the film immediately after the 'To be or not to be' in the crypt, needs a change of location. Hamlet's reference to 'this most excellent canopy the air, look you, this brave o'erhanging firmament' makes the choice of an outdoor location a natural one. Green slopes and the porch of a picturesquely primitive tavern form the backdrop of a dynamically edited scene in which an aggressive Hamlet exposes the double dealings of his former friends. The appearance of the troupe of players takes us logically on to the next location – the vast courtyard of Elsinore Castle, with Hamlet entering merrily in motley dress along with the players. In spite of the deletion of the entire theatrical banter of Acts II and III, we are given an immediate sense of Hamlet's familiarity with the world of acting. As in Act I, sc.2 (with Hamlet observing Claudius and his mother kissing from above), the essentially *operatic* space of the courtyard, with its massive flight of steps and windows on high, is used to create a pattern of significant gazes and reaction shots between Gertrude (in the window), Claudius and Polonius (on the steps), Hamlet, and Rosencrantz and Guildenstern (significantly scurrying between Hamlet and Claudius) which speaks volumes.

Ultimately then, place *frames* action in Zeffirelli's *Hamlet*, as in Zeffirelli's films generally. Place does not, as in Brooks' *King Lear*, in Kozintsev's *Hamlet*, or in Kurosawa's *Throne of Blood*, take on special *significance* on a par with character and action. As Pauline Kael puts it, quite simply: '[in Zeffirelli] the realistic locations are used like parts of a stage.'[10]

Zeffirelli's Cinematic Strategies

The 'naturalism', poetic or otherwise, of Zeffirelli's *Hamlet* leaves little scope for heavily foregrounded cinematic features. Characters, actions, and objects are essentially *denotative* rather than connotative, and cinematic features such as camera movement, distance and angle, cutting, lighting and sound track essentially *anchor* or *enhance* already established signification. To give one obvious example: A disembodied, floating camera as used in Olivier's 1948 *Hamlet* is inconceivable in this film, because the film offers no scope for a sustained symbolic reading, firmly grounded as it is in the colourful, concrete reality of 'Baroque' naturalism. The flying camera of the opening scene of this *Hamlet* does not present a point of view within the diegesis, but serves simply as a melodramatic enhancement of the imposing orchestration of the scene as a whole. A further example: the neat overlap of the shadow of Hamlet/ Olivier's head with Yorick's skull in the Gravedigger Scene of Olivier's 1948 *Hamlet* would be highly unlikely in Zeffirelli – it would be too much of a foregrounding of intentional design to fit into the overall naturalistic approach.

Alas, poor Yorick –
Zeffirelli's Baroque naturalism lets the symbols speak for themselves.

By the same token, the low-angle closeup of Gibson's face as he moves into 'What piece of work is a man ...' (II.2. 295-310) is not a metaphorical composition, and in this I find myself in disagreement with David Impastato,

125

quoted above, who argues that the use of light, and particularly direct sunlight, is the organising metaphor of Zeffirelli's film:

> In his recent production of *Hamlet*, Franco Zeffirelli offers a unique directorial vision that emerges with authority and finds striking cinematic expression for Shakespeare's theatrical text. A unity of image and idea consistently governs all elements of the film, from costuming and photography to characterization and *mise en scène*. What sets this film apart visually from any previous adaptation of *Hamlet* is the presence of direct sunlight, even in the greater part of the interiors.[11]

There are no *organising* metaphors in Zeffirelli's *Hamlet*, for the simple reason that Zeffirelli does not provide the scope for this type of meta-level of signification. This does not mean that there are no recurrent images or signifiers. Sunlight and darkness, classic Manichaean oppositions of melodrama, figure prominently, as in Hamlet's two major soliloquies, 'O, that this too, too sullied flesh' and 'To be or not to be'.

'O that this too too sullied flesh...' is spoken in Hamlet's dark, musty study. As he gets to the line: 'Fie on't, ah fie, 'tis an unweeded garden/ that grows to seed' he gets up and walks to the window overlooking the courtyard, from which voices and noise are heard. Half in shadow, half in the sun, he continues his soliloquy, looking down on Claudius and his mother, kissing as they prepare for a ride on horseback. Zeffirelli has him finish off the soliloquy with the phrase: 'Frailty, thy name is woman' – a punch line which sets up a fine match cut to the following scene, with Ophelia in her room, saying goodbye to her brother Laertes. In the 'To be or not to be' crypt scene, the stairway and a skylight grill provide the sunlight. Hamlet meanders about the crypt uttering his famous lines, with sarcophaguses, skulls and bones *enhancing* the mood and theme of mortality. At one point only is there a clear shift between darkness and sunlight, when he moves forward and the light suddenly illuminates his face as he gets to: 'And thus the native hue of resolution/ Is sicklied o'er with the pale cast of thought'.

The third, and most obvious use of sunlight is in Act V, sc.2, with Hamlet and Horatio, immediately before the final fencing scene, watching the setting sun, and Hamlet saying: 'If it be now, 'tis not to come; if it be not to come, it will be now; if it be not now, yet it will come. The readiness is all'.

However, a close look at all three examples will yield nothing in terms of sunlight as inscribed in a overriding system of binary signification. Obviously, the early Hamlet in particular is a moody, indoor-type of person, in contrast to the lively, horseback-riding Claudius and Gertrude. But Hamlet in the exterior scenes is not really any different. The sunlight is inhabited equally by everyone in the play. In other words, the chiaroscuro effects are simply *local* intensifiers, making for interesting photography, but essentially 'part of the world' – resolutely *not* foregrounding themselves as an autonomous system of signification. And a setting sun is a setting sun is a setting sun.

Much the same applies to Zeffirelli's use of music. Perhaps with a view to the classically sombre nature of the subject matter, and to avoid the epithet 'operatic', Zeffirelli chose Ennio Morricone, well known for his radically minimalist score of Sergio Leone's *Once upon a Time in the West*, a dramatic departure compared to, for example, the sensuously overblown Nino Rota score of *Romeo and Juliet*. The Morricone music has no pretentions beyond enhancing. Extremely low-key, for long stretches even absent, the music is nevertheless extremely effective as enhancer and moodsetter. The music never competes, or is contrapuntal to the words, but it frequently sets in as a particular scene intensifies – often, as in television drama, accompanied by zoom-ins and closeups. Lyrical passages are often supported by only a single, unobtrusive instrument playing – usually an oboe or a cello. Longer dramatic passages are sustained by a low orchestral ostinato of modulating chords. The only obtrusive use of music in the film is in the opening sequence, when the camera approach to Elsinore is accompanied by 'courtly', early Baroque-like music, blending into the organ music of the crypt scene. And, of course, in the final scene, as the camera is raised upward and away, when we hear the swell not of Baroque but of Romantic orchestral music, underscoring not the catharsis, but the emotional expressivity of the finale.

The only formal cinematic feature of Zeffirelli's *Hamlet* with which an attempt is made to create an overarching formal paradigm of signification is the *tinting*. Zeffirelli works two special types of coloration: Warm amber tinting (a favourite of his), and a contrastive cold greyish blue. Amber is associated with indoor candle-lit rooms, and the greyish blue with outdoor sombre scenes, e.g. those involving Hamlet and his father's ghost. The contrast is made dramatically in Act I, Sc.4, with Hamlet outside on the battlements looking down through the skylight at the amber-coloured banquet scene in the great hall of the castle, reflecting:

'This heavy-headed revel east and west
Makes us traduc'd and tax'd of other nations –
They clepe us drunkards, and with swinish phrase
Soil our addition; and indeed it takes
From our achievements, though perform'd at height
The pith and marrow of our attribute.' (I.4. 17-22)

However, Zeffirelli makes further, and problematic, use of this distinction between amber and greyish blue to create a point of view distinction in the closet scene with the Queen. The appearance of the ghost to Hamlet is presented in greyish blue, whereas the Queen's point of view shot of the doorway where the ghost is supposed to be is presented in the amber tinting in which the rest of the scene is shot. In other words, Hamlet's subjective, potentially deranged vision is identified with the greyish blue tinting, and this is confusing (a) because Zeffirelli's previous use of greyish blue, e.g in the first ghost scene, was not subject-bound and did not indicate any lack of 'reality' in the ghost, and (b) because the use of greyish blue is not restricted to scenes in which Hamlet is present. By the same token, amber tinting has no stable connotations: it is used with the banquet scene, with Ophelia's room, massively with the Queen's closet, and with Claudius sealing letters; and there is an abundance of amber light emanating from the doorway in the outdoor parting scene between Gertrude and Hamlet in Act IV.

The use of tinting is problematic in a way in which the use of sunlight/lack of the same is not, because it is used *both* as a formal system of signification (in the closet scene) and as a general feature of enhancement. As I have pointed out, Zeffirelli really cannot have it both ways without creating what can only be described as an unintentional confusion concerning the nature of both the ghost and Hamlet's grasp of reality.

Casting and Directing

Casting and directing of actors are areas frequently neglected in academic film scholarship. Directing is a collective process of give and take in which the attribution of credit or blame is difficult, even to the people involved. Casting, by the same token, while obviously a manifestation of the governing *vision* of producer/director, involves so much else in addition : availability, budget and box office considerations, existing personal relationships, plus the elusive affective relations between well-known actors and cinema audiences.

> The greatest innovations of this production lay in unifying words and stage-business, and in making the actors' speech as lively and fluent as their physical action. The result was that the dialogue did not appear the effect of study and care, but the natural idiom of the characters in the particular situations. It is a long time since Shakespeare's text has been so enfranchised.[12]

These words refer to Zeffirelli's theatrical production of *Romeo and Juliet* in 1960 at the Old Vic in London, but they might equally be applied to his *Hamlet*. Zeffirelli's capacity for *naturalizing* Shakespeare is evidenced in all of his Shakespearean work. He is primarily a *communicator* rather than an *interpreter*. Individual direction and a sense of the narrative dynamics of drama are the essential clues to the success of this production. It is the ease and the fluency of execution rather than the profundity of vision which are the redeeming qualities of this *Hamlet*.

Zeffirelli has a track record of spectacular casting, and *Hamlet* is no exception. The international mix of seasoned Shakespeareans and popular screen personalities in the casting of *Hamlet* makes for a width of appeal which positions the film as a mainstream production rather than an art cinema one. As indicated by my introductory quotation, Zeffirelli clearly wants to *transcend* what he sees as the artificial division between the 'serious' and the 'popular', just as Shakespeare is generally perceived to have transcended this division. The juxtaposition of high Shakespeare and low commercial filming in itself points to this; casting is another, and obvious way of making this point.

Gertrude (Glenn Close) and Hamlet (Mel Gibson). The fatal Oedipal attraction.

The bankability of Mel 'Mad Max' Gibson and Glenn 'Fatal Attraction' Close are balanced against the cultured Britishness of Alan Bates, Ian Holm, newcomer Helena Bonham-Carter and, as Ghost, veteran Shakespearean Paul Scofield, known in particular from the title role of Peter Brook's *King Lear*.

As an ensemble, the cast display a uniformly high professional level of acting in *Hamlet*. Frank Kermode, in his 'Commentary on *Hamlet*', puts it even more strongly: 'I don't think I have ever heard the lines of the play spoken by an entire cast with such authority and resource as in this film.'[13]

The casting of Close and Bonham-Carter in particular indicates fresh approaches, Close being cast very much in the role of the sincere, not too clever, foolishly infatuated mature woman, and Bonham-Carter playing an Ophelia with a mind of her own, combined with an intriguing blend of confused innocence and erotic awareness, without the palely loitering quality of, for example, Olivier's Jean Simmons.

129

However, the overall quality of any *Hamlet* production hinges on two crucial points: one, the conception and casting of Hamlet himself, and two, a cohesive *vision* of what should be perceived to emerge as happening in the play. Mel Gibson as an actor quite simply has a limited range of expression – you can only roll your eyes and shake your head so many times in the same film. This limited range, however, is largely offset by a surplus of vitality and vigorous movement, and an admirable clarity of diction. On the second count, however, Zeffirelli, is found wanting: as instanced in the above, there is a lack of governing vision in this production. As in *Romeo and Juliet*, Zeffirelli has a sophisticated sense of *texture*,i.e. of mood, decor, costume, setting and staging. But the *structure*, i.e. the developmental dynamics of the play, are unclear. In *Romeo and Juliet* we were given a Romeo whose *development* from superficial courtier and womanizer into a real human being in love was largely ignored in favour of the melodrama of the love plot. In *Hamlet* we are presented with a character whose motives are not complex, but unclear, up against an uncle who is not sufficiently villainous to provide that motivation, and a Polonius who is somehow neither the bureaucratic mastermind nor the loquacious comic relief, but somewhere in between. *Power*, in other words, is diffusely conceived at Zeffirelli's Elsinore.So, as a consequence, is the frustration of *powerlessness* which is such an important ingredient of the central domain of the play: Hamlet's state of mind.

In the final analysis, the Zeffirelli *Hamlet* lacks an overall sense of direction, in every sense of the phrase. Melodrama as a point of entry to *Hamlet* makes interesting sense from a theoretical point of view. However, without an overall sense of the consequences to texture and structure of such an approach, the result, however entertaining and glamorous, remains unconvincing. Laurence Olivier, with becoming if unjustified modesty called his 1948 film 'an Essay in Hamlet'.[14] Zeffirelli, in an interview, summarized his approach to *Hamlet* in the following words: 'I simply put the mechanics of popular theatre in motion.'[15]

Notes

1. T.S. Eliot, 'Hamlet and his Problems', in T.S. Eliot, *The Sacred Wood* (London: Methuen, 1960), p.101.
2. Ibid., p. 102.
3. Peter Brooks, *The Melodramatic Imagination* (New Haven: Yale University Press, 1976), p. 15.
4. *Hamlet*, ed. Harold Jenkins (London: Routledge 1989, The Arden Edition). All further references are to this edition and are included in the text.
5. Jonathan Romney, Review of Zeffirelli's *Hamlet*, *Sight and Sound*, May 1991, p.49.

6. In this Zeffirelli follows the 1948 *Hamlet*, in which Olivier and Alan Dent cut 'How all occasions do inform against me'. In Alan Dent, ed., *Hamlet: The Film and the Play* (London: World Film Publications 1948), Alan Dent notes: 'It proved intractable as cinematic material, and Olivier found it impossibly static in screen terms, though he hated to have to part with it as much as I did' (No pagination).

7. Pauline Kael, *Going Steady* (Boston: Little, Brown and Co., 1968).

8. *Shakespeare on Film Newsletter*, April 1992 and Dec. 1991.

9. David Impastato, 'Zeffirelli's Hamlet and the Baroque', *Shakespeare on Film Newsletter*, April 1992, p. 1.

10. *Going Steady*, p. 155.

11. David Impastato, 'Zeffirelli's Hamlet: Sunlight Makes Meaning', *Shakespeare on Film Newsletter*, December 1991, p. 1.

12. See Murray Biggs, 'He's going to his Mother's Closet: Hamlet and Gertrude on Screen', *Shakespeare Survey*, 45 (Cambridge: Cambridge University Press, 1993). Biggs, in comparing the 1980 BBC *Hamlet* with the Olivier and Zeffirelli *Hamlets*, makes the general point: 'It is a weakness of the BBC production that the ghost is presented only from Hamlet's point of view. The camera ought also to show us, as it does under both Olivier's and Zeffirelli's direction, that from Gertrude's perspective there is nothing to see; it is what she says, at line 132. The queen is not simply deprived of her senses here, or lying about what she does or does not see. It is her moral obliquity that obscures her vision, just as Hamlet's enhanced sensibility enables his' (p. 61).

13. John Russell Brown, *Shakespeare's Plays in Performance*, (London: Edward Arnold, 1966), p. 170.

14. Kermode, Frank, 'A Commentary on Hamlet', *Film Education Study Guide*, (London: BFI, 1992), p. 2.

15. *The Film Hamlet: a Record of its Production*, ed. Brenda Cross, (London: The Saturn Press, 1948), p. 12.

16. Angie Errigo, 'The Italian Job', *Empire*, May 1991, p. 47.

'Knowing I Lov'd My Books': Shakespeare, Greenaway, and the Prosperous Dialectics of Word and Image

Claus Schatz-Jacobsen

1. Introduction. *The Tempest*: Page, Stage and Screen

How does a film director approach a play by Shakespeare such as *The Tempest* with the intention of adapting it to the cinema? By disregarding the differences between literary and cinematic discourse and by 'forgetting' that what he proposes to do is to translate the meaning of the text without loss or gain from its original medium, that of words in sequence, into a derived medium, that of moving images? He can do so by pretending that the essence of the play lies in its epic dimension, in that capacity for telling a story that roams freely over time and space which the film can handle as well as, if not better than, narrative literary texts, in which case the play seems to reveal its true nature only as a novel turned filmscript. Or he can remain the theatrical fundamentalist and insist on the dramatic dimension of the play while rendering it as filmed theatre, in which case he accepts the conventionalities and the spatio-temporal constraints of theatrical productions. Still, either way differences are overcome as film and play meet halfway, each contributing something uniquely its own to the final, synthesizing result.

Or, alternatively, he can adapt the play to cinema by respecting the inherently different ontological natures of the two media and by recreating the image within the domain staked out by the words on the page (and vice versa), but without reducing them to the self-identity of a transcendental meaning, independent of the medium that communicates it.[1]

Judging by the number of more or less felicitous cinematic adaptations to which *The Tempest* has been subjected over the years, e.g. Fred McLeod's science-fictionalization *Forbidden Planet* (1955), George Schaefer's little-known adaptation from 1959, which hovers undecidably between slapstick comedy and serious revenge drama, and Derek Jarman's irrevently gothicized *Tempest* (1982), the majority of directors opt for one of the first, 'synthesizing' approaches. This applies in particular to the adaptation of *The Tempest* from 1988 in the 'BBC Shakespeare' series, which reproduces the source with such respect for the Shakespearean spirit of the play that it can offer to pay no more than lip service to the cinematic medium, thus becoming virtually uninteresting as a *visual* experience.

What I drew up as the alternative to the 'synthesizing' approaches may have sounded slightly vague and without address to any particular director or film. Such would indeed be the proper response to my words, for they apply exclusively to *Prospero's Books* (1991), the idiosyncratic vision of *The Tempest* by Peter Greenaway, English film director-painter, a cinematic version of a literary work which is unique in confronting squarely the fundamental question of the different modes of existence of literary texts and cinematic images. *Prospero's Books* – the title indicating, says Greenaway, that 'it is not a straight attempt to reproduce a familiar text'[2] – is undoubtedly one of the most outstandingly personal and uniquely experimental contributions to the history of Shakespearean films. It conjures up a high-Renaissance universe *en miniature* which bears clearly legible traces of Greenaway's pictorial imagination while rendering the literary source with astonishing fidelity. Whatever the nature of Greenaway's deliberations concerning how to approach *The Tempest*, *Prospero's Books* is unique in its respect for the literality of Shakespeare's text, in the original sense of the word *literal* as pertaining to the letter, being as it were a literal rewriting of *The Tempest*. Greenaway himself comments in a book which grew out of his work on the film that

> the project deliberately emphasises and celebrates the text as text, as the master material on which all the magic, illusion and deception of the play is based. Words making text, and text making pages, and pages making books from which knowledge is fabricated in pictorial form – these are the persistently forefronted characteristics.[3]

The finally realized version of *Prospero's Books* owes its existence to Greenaway, but the seminal idea of filming the play is due to Sir John Gielgud, who plays Prospero. While working with Greenaway on *A TV Dante*, Gielgud presented to him the idea of filming *The Tempest* with himself as Prospero, an idea which he had nourished for several years and which he had already suggested to Bergman, Kurosawa, and Fellini, among others. Greenaway embraced the idea and quickly won Gielgud over to his own matrix for the film. In designing the role of Prospero specifically for Gielgud, Greenaway drew for the many obvious analogies in *Prospero's Books* as between leading actor and main character on Gielgud's 'powerful and authoritative ability to speak text – verse and prose',[4] his age, and on the fact that, having played Prospero several times in his immensely long theatrical career and being indeed the paragon of British 20th-century Shakespeare acting, Gielgud verily *incarnates* the character of Prospero.

2. *The Tempest* and the Changing Winds of Reception

The Tempest, literary historians generally agree, is Shakespeare's last play, written and first performed at Court in 16ll. However, it was never published in Shakespeare's own lifetime, and appeared in print only in the so-called First Folio, John Heminge and Henry Condell's *Mr. William Shakespeare's Comedies, Histories & Tragedies* (1623), where, significantly, it was given pride of place, occupying as it does the first nineteen pages.

It is interesting that, in contrast to the great majority of Shakespeare's plays, no single source or intended meaning of *The Tempest* has been unearthed. Comparative scholars have suggested a number of possible influences and partial sources, English and foreign, popular and learned, literary, philosophical and theological, not to mention a welter of analogies, textual echoes, and allusions, but the fact remains that as it stands, the play forms an exceptionally rich miscellany of the traditional and the original.[5]

While frustrating historical and textual critics anxious to reconstruct or recapture the origin of the play in the form of the historically correct text or the most authentic meaning, the fact that *The Tempest* has not yielded its secret has positively stimulated other critics to pore instead over the possibilities of reading into the richly ambiguous verbal texture of the play all manner of hidden, allegorical significance.[6]

G. Wilson Knight is one allegorical reader, heir to the tradition of reading *The Tempest* as autobiography, which reaches back to early 20th-century critics such as Harris, Middleton Murry, and Jones, through the Victorians Dowden and Swinburne, to Coleridge, a Romantic originator of that tradition. However, there is one decisive difference between Knight's autobiographical reading and its earlier precedents: Knight sees *The Tempest* as *artistic*, not as *spiritual* autobiography. In 'The Shakespearian Superman: a study of *The Tempest*' (1947), he elaborates on insights reaped in his brief, earlier essay 'Myth and Miracle' (1929), where he refutes source- and intention-hunting criticism of Shakespeare. His point in the later essay is that Shakespeare's last plays, which in 'Myth and Miracle' he had described as 'the culmination of a series which starts about the middle of Shakespeare's writing career',[7] are peculiar in seizing on poetry itself for their effects, a tendency which is taken to an extreme in *The Tempest*. Devoid of all sources except the autonomous world of poetry, *The Tempest* is 'an interpretation of Shakespeare's world', Prospero being a 'composite of many Shakespearian heroes'.[8] Knight's explication brings out the many intertextual references in *The Tempest* to earlier Shakespeare plays, concluding on the allegorical note of Prospero as a reflection of Shakespeare himself and the play as dramatized self-representation. Hence *The Tempest* reads like a tour of Shakespeare's dramatic work with Prospero as guide, a final *summum* and distillation of a tempestuous life devoted to the art of the theatre. This reading is borne out in particular by its central exhibit, the epilogue of the play, which conflates Prospero and Shakespeare in a joint farewell to the *dramatis personae* of *The Tempest* and to the art of the theatre, actors and audience included:

Now my charms are all o'erthrown,
And what strength I have's mine own,
Which is most faint: now, t'is true,
I must be here confin'd by you,
Or sent to Naples. Let me not,
Since I have my dukedom got,
And pardon'd the deceiver, dwell
In this bare island by your spell;
But release me from my bands
With the help of your good hands:
Gentle breath of yours my sails
Must fill, or else my project fails,
Which was to please. Now I want
Spirits to enforce, Art to enchant;
And my ending is despair,
Unless I be reliev'd by prayer,
Which pierces so, that it assaults
Mercy itself, and frees all faults.
　　　As you from crimes would pardon'd be,
　　　Let your indulgence set me free.[9]

3. *Prospero's Books*: The Theatre of Books

Prospero's Books is clearly of a piece with this tradition in Shakespeare criticism, which still provides no more than a point of departure for the magisterial superimposition on the 'naked' text of Greenaway's own drama of pivotal, centrally informing ideas.

The first and most central idea, which takes off from the above-mentioned critical tradition while linking it with the post-Modern literary *topos* of 'the truth of the page',[10] the portrayal of the author in the act of writing, is to blur the ontological boundary line between life and art, between the historical Shakespeare and his character, Prospero. The latter is represented as a Shakespearean *alter ego*, sitting in his study on the desert island writing the play into which he projects himself as leading actor and, less conspicuously, as director (roles also adopted from time to time by the historical Shakespeare).

The resultant Prospero-Shakespeare figure is the demiurge and master-magician of his projected universe, creator and manipulator of those imaginary characters which are conjured up by sheer verbal force to be the willing instruments of his carefully contrived and plotted desire for revenge.

This symbolic exchange of identities as between Prospero and Shakespeare is the stepping-stone for Greenaway's boldest conceit in *Prospero's Books*, that of letting Prospero-Gielgud speak all the roles, which turns the film quite literally into a 'reading' of the play. This is done by means of overdubbing, the obviously 'contrived' character of which lends support to the essentially imaginary atmosphere of the film, with Prospero's voice echoing back from all corners of his solipsistic universe.

In the certain hope of dynastic succession in the houses of Milan and Naples Prospero unites Ferdinand and Miranda

The second structuring idea of *Prospero's Books* takes its point of departure in the brief mention in *The Tempest* of those books which Prospero was allowed by his loyal councellor, Gonzalo, to take with him when, twelve years prior to the action, he was exiled from his Milanese dukedom with his daughter Miranda:

so, of his gentleness,
Knowing I lov'd my books, he furnished me
From mine own library with volumes that
I prize above my dukedom.   (I.2.165-68)

These apochryphal volumes, 24 in Greenaway's count, have been 'reconstructed' by Greenaway with all the ingenuity that advanced video-recording and editing techniques, including high-definition television (HDTV) and computer-paintbox graphics, have placed into his hands. Accompanied by the comments of a voice-over, the books punctuate the film, and function as a counterpoint to the dramatic story, much like chapter headings in a novel. While being coterminous with the two-hour duration of the film, the volumes constitute a Renaissance encyclopedia of Western civilization, symbol of its vast bookish culture, a library containing two millenia of accumulated arts and sciences: medicine, architecture, mechanics, geometry, music, language, mythology, etc. By means of sophisticated video post-production techniques of superimposition and animation, the volumes come alive on the screen: 'when the pages are opened in this book', says the voice-over about *A Memoria Technica called Architecture and other Music*, 'plans and diagrams spring up fully formed. There are definitive models of buildings, constantly shaded by moving cloud-shadow. Lights flicker in nocturnal urban landscapes, and music is played in the halls and towers' – and what is more, the unfolded model building instantly metamorphoses into the actual stage set of the film's next scene. Vesalius's lost *Anatomy of Birth*, 'heretical and disturbing', says the voice-over, is 'full of descriptive drawings of the workings of the human body, which, when the pages open, move, and throb, and bleed' – and disgorge bloody organs! In *A Book of Games* chessmen move across a chessboard, in *A Book of Colours* the colours shade into one another incessantly, in *A Bestiary of Past, Present and Future Animals* the pages are littered with animals, and so on without end.

In the epilogue Prospero lives up to his promise, made at the beginning of Act V when he realizes that he commands the stage, of drowning his books. Divested of his magic robe, he surrenders to the water his beloved books, including the significant volume 23, *A Book of Thirty-Five Plays* – 'a thick printed volume of plays, dated 1623. There are 35 plays in the book, and room for one more. Nineteen pages have been left for its inclusion, right at the front of the book, just after the preface' that is, Heminge and Condell's First Folio – and the final, 24th volume, 'the 36th play, *The Tempest*'. Concludes the voice-over, 'whilst the other volumes have been drowned and destroyed, we still have these last two books, safely fished from the sea' – as indeed they are, by the 'foul slave', Caliban, in the finale of the film.

3.1. Prospero and The Realm of the Educated Imagination

While Greenaway seems to have cast his Prospero in the image of the Renaissance painter Giovanni Bellini's portrait of the *Doge Loredano*, with his characteristic headgear and florid robe, so the physical setting of *Prospero's Books* is cast, not as a humble cell, as it has often been represented in the theatre and on film, but as an intricately departmentalized Renaissance *palazzo*, complete with Roman bath-house and library – indeed, with all the architectural paraphernalia of the Renaissance mind's rage for order and harmony, the physical evidence of its three-dimensional, central perspectivist mastery of space.[11]

The mise-en-scene of *Prospero's Books* is far from insignificant, but the kind of 'reality-effect' to which setting, acting, and lighting lend themselves is one of imaginative realism rather than of crudely historical realism, for the 'real' setting is the internal palace of Prospero's imagination, a place

> whose references are forged by an unhappy scholar recreating a little Renaissance kingdom far from Europe. It is a place where the indigenous spirits are persuaded to impersonate classical mythological figures, where Prospero dresses like a Venetian doge, where Caliban dances and there are four Ariels to represent the elements, and the world is appreciated and referenced with the architecture, paintings and classical literature Prospero has imported[12]

– expanding as it does beyond the boundaries of the physical universe.[13] Its Renaissance topicality notwithstanding, the setting of the film is therefore as 'naked' as the Elizabethan apron stage, a metaphor for space in general rather than a realistic – metonymic – representation of any one particular space.

This type of stage provides the constant theatrical reference point for Jan Kott's discussion in 'Prospero's Staff' of the geography of *The Tempest*, which can be brought to bear with equal force on *Prospero's Books*. Kott invites his reader to look at the island more closely, providing as it does the scene of the drama proper. He makes a token attempt to locate it in the physical world, linking his argument with one of the assumed sources of *The Tempest*, the travel reports of the discovery of the New World across the Atlantic, but he concludes that 'it is useless ... to look for the longitude and latitude of Prospero's island',[14] which, defying all laws of nature, is out of time. For the fact is, says Kott, that 'the island does not exist. Prospero's island is either the world, or the stage. To the Elizabethans it was all the same; the stage was the world, and the world was the stage'.[15]

3.2. Prospero and the Framing Power of the Voice

I have suggested that *Prospero's Books* follows the general narrative of its source with astonishing fidelity. Providing as it were avenues to the play's past and future, its prologue and epilogue frame the four-hour story 'proper' of how Prospero's thirst for revenge over his enemies works towards its inevitable end, of how he counters the twin assaults on his absolute supremacy of the island, and of how he finally decides to forgive his enemies and acquit them of their misdeeds while asking to be set free in his turn.

Like Botticelli's *Birth of Venus*, the prologue of *Prospero's Books* is born of water, or rather of a confluence of waters. What seems at first sight to be the montage-like juxtaposition of apparently independent, discontinuous sequences of shots – of the close-up of continuously dripping water; of the water which surrounds the Prospero of the establishing shot, standing in his Roman bath by a floating table on which rests the *Book of Water*; of the close-up of the ink-pot in which the hand of Prospero dips his pen to write the word 'Boatswain'; of Prospero's unseen bodily fluids, source of the tempest of his passions – all of these elements turn out towards the end of the prologue to be so many tributaries issuing in the flood of the speaking, writing, and staging of *The Tempest*. The prologue presents the several streams, the outer influences and inner promptings, which intersect in Prospero's imagination – that well from which, on the spur of a moment's play with a word and a toy vessel, he improvises the play, raises the tempest.

Prospero is the omnipotent author-creator, the privileged locus of the intention, governing idea and overall meaning of his play. From him emanate the recitation, writing and dramatic rehearsal of his desire for revenge and for the restoration of his legal title to the dukedom of Milan. All the *characters*[16] of *Prospero's Books* read like emblematic inscriptions in the physical world of Prospero's unbounded power. Their presences depend on Prospero as the solid foundation of the game in which they are caught up, as the intention of which they are the expression, as the unshakeable, self-identical ground from which the beginning, middle and end of their temporary physical existence is staked out. Prospero is the embodiment of the ideal man, *l'uomo universale*, of Renaissance Humanism, a unity of philosopher, politician, and poet, the new dynamic centre of the universe who arrogates to himself the attributes that medieval Scholastic philosophers had ascribed to God. His voice being possessed of such awesome power that by emulating the divine Logos, the creative word of God, he can body forth his enemies while keeping them in a state of dazed death-in-life, he is the incarnation of what the French thinker Jacques Derrida has instructed us in *Of Grammatology* and elsewhere to identify – and criticize – as the 'logocentric' tradition of Western metaphysics, the ever-recurrent orientation toward 'an order of meaning – thought, truth, reason, logic, the Word – conceived as existing in itself, as foundation'.[17]

Logocentrism merges, argues Derrida, with the 'metaphysics of presence', with 'the determination through history of the meaning of being in general as *presence*',[18] with the naming, that is, of an entity which exists in originary, fully self-present plenitude as ontological foundation and inalienable part of being.

Throughout the history of philosophy, logocentrism has coincided with 'phonocentrism', with the tradition of privileging speech over writing while condemning the latter to a secondary status as a degraded representation of the purity of the voice, irreparably fallen into exteriority, into the condition of the material. The only philosophically acceptable kind of writing is what Derrida calls a 'restricted writing', which corresponds with all empirically determined systems of writing, be they ideographic, pictographic, hieroglyphic, or alphabetical, and which submits to the servile task of representing speech while letting itself be bound within the covers of a book. Therefore the logocentric-phonocentric tradition in Western philosophy is also the history and metaphysics of the book and its author, the author being the name of the book's authoritative master and owner, the instance guaranteeing that the writing contained within its covers remains linked to a voice and is therefore ultimately decipherable and meaningful.

The name of the bibliophile Prospero is indeed the name of the author and proper owner of books, the name of the Proper, the author-ity, founding principle and centre of the imaginary universe which he projects from his safely ensconced position in his Renaissance study. In immediate proximity with the mind as the locus of meaning and intention, Derrida's 'transcendental signified', Prospero's voice is infinitely capable of projecting what, except for itself, would be theatrical dumb-shows of power, a dissemination of dramatic tableaux, mounted in frames of one kind or another. Frames are generated *ad infinitum* in the form of window-frames, colonnades, pages from books, *passes partouts*, and miniature proscenium arches, not to mention the frequent superimposed images, piled layer upon layer, each framing the next. The framing-devices in *Prospero's Books* are indeed so numerous as to make of the film one great effort of *theatricalization* on Prospero's part, of displaying his infinite power over the material world as Baconian philosopher (mind → matter), as Macchiavellian statesman (sovereign → subject), and as Shakespearean dramatist (author → work).

Analogous to the viewing frame of the draughtsman, Mr. Neville, in Greenaway's first feature film *The Draughtman's Contract* (1982), the frames in *Prospero's Books* are of vital importance as testifying to Prospero's Nietzschean will-to-power over his universe. For the frame is a figure of epistemology, the instrument and specular image of a mind which reasons *more geometrico* and which, bent on a totalizing grasp of the material world, is characterized, partly by what it *includes*, what it will allow within the frame, and by what it *excludes*, partly by the three-dimensional ordering of what is admitted. Therefore it is no accident that Prospero's desire for revenge is represented as theatrical

140

performance, for it is in the nature of the theatre to be the place where, in an act of representation which testifies to the sovereignty of director and spectator alike, objects and characters are represented and made visible in a certain ordered space.[19] Prospero remains a figure of displaced theology in this theatre, the theatre of representation, a figure of the author-God, hovering above the world of his creation, who can be approached *speculatively*, by way of the contemplative gaze that recognizes the creator in the mirror (*speculum*) of the created universe.[20]

Prospero's universe of representations by voice, written text, and theatrical performance, being in the final account a giant hall of mirrors, complete with a very *Book of Mirrors*, therefore comes down finally to a single gesture of dramatic *self-representation*. Wherever Prospero turns in this realm of the imaginary and looks out from the palace of his mind, he sees his own specular image reflected in mirrors; indeed, he sees the entire universe as created *in his own image*. Hence the images of which his universe is composed take on the same quality as 'such stuff/ As dreams are made on' (IV.i.156-57), that immaterial, insubstantial, finally ideal quality with which, throughout the logocentric-phonocentric history of Western philosophy, the voice has been privileged as the natural medium of thought, the medium in which it can shine through in immediate, uncontaminated self-presence.

A Book of Water.

Text, theatre, and cinema are infinitely malleable media, and thus even the dominant figure of the cinematic rhetoric of *Prospero's Books*, the superimposed shot, itself seems to aid Prospero in being visibly present in all corners of his universe. Superimposition has the effect of depicting the abysmal depth and range of Prospero's mind, his command of time and space, of presence and absence, of past and future. Ontological difference is invariably overcome and sublimated by superimposition, reduced to the self-identity of the *eidos*, for instance in one of the collage-like, literally composed tableaux of the prologue. A medium close-up of Prospero the actor-director, rehearsing the opening line of the play, 'Boatswain', is superimposed on a close-up of the parchment on which the hand of Prospero the author is writing that very word. What is noticeable about the shot as a whole is the transparency of the superimposition – its frame is clearly distinguishable, and yet the background shot is no less clearly 'readable', even literally so, as the emblematic inscription of the mind that hovers above it. Thus cinematic superimposition 'mirrors' the superimposition of Prospero's mind on the physical world.

3.3. Prospero's Conversion by Writing

I have already revealed that what starts out as a tragedy of revenge turns into a comedy of forgiveness and reconciliation at that significant point in the story when, prevailed upon by Ariel, Prospero sets the creatures of his imagination free and pardons them their wrongs by giving them a voice and a life of their own. Let us recount what leads up to this nodal scene, which provides the climactic turning-point of the film.

Finding that Ariel has usurped his writing-desk to add to the manuscript a line of heartfelt concern for Prospero's victims ('Your charm so strongly works 'em,/ That if you now beheld them, your affections/ Would become tender'; V.1.17-19), the latter decides to forego all further punishment of them:

> Though with their high wrongs I am struck to th'quick,
> Yet with my nobler reason 'gainst my fury
> Do I take part: the rarer action is
> In virtue than in vengeance: they being penitent,
> The sole drift of my purpose doth extend
> Not a frown further.   (V.1.20-30)

Immediately all Prospero's books are closed up, only to be consumed by fire and surrendered to water, and while the stage is being set for the great reconciliation, Prospero gives the speech in which he promises to abjure his rough magic;

>   and, when I have requir'd
> Some heavenly music, – which even now I do, –
> To work mine end upon their senses, that
> This airy charm is for, I'll break my staff,
> Bury it certain fathoms in the earth,
> And deeper than did ever plummet sound
> I'll drown my book.   (V.1.51-57)

This is the symbolic death of Prospero as author, the crucial point at which he voluntarily renounces his authority over his projected universe and his position as privileged, transcendental writing subject. But why this sudden change of mind and heart on Prospero's part? The answer is very simple: because he becomes morally and aesthetically involved with the characters that he has bodied forth. Prospero is finally stigmatized as the flawed hero at the point when he allows himself to become touched by the seductively beautiful italics, inscribed in his own hand on yellowish parchment, which are thrown into relief by Ariel's uncouth marginal note, as well as by the painful, morally de-graded position to which he has brought his enemies, that is, by the otherness and starkly opaque materiality of his subject characters.

However, the essence of *Prospero's Books* is not psychological drama, it does not explore its characters in depth, and therefore Prospero's change of mind and heart is less important than its effects: the release of his enemies and the ceremonial destruction of his books. It is significant that what is irre-trievably lost in this great conflagration of art are the twenty-two volumes, the shaping influences from which, as vehicles of clasical learning, Prospero created his own universe. What survives, on the other hand, rescued from the sea by Caliban, are the text of *The Tempest* and the First Folio, Heminge and Condell's *Comedies, Histories & Tragedies*, whose only frame of reference is the individual life of their author, readable mainly in the biographical context of the man that lives and suffers as his mind creates.

4. Conclusion

Whence the elective affinity between Greenaway and the Prospero-Shakespeare that he recreates from *The Tempest*? I suggested one of the reasons earlier when I mentioned the many analogies in the film, deliberately 'planted' by Greenaway, between Gielgud and the character(s) that he plays in the film. Prospero's meta-dramatic farewell in the epilogue to his audience, to the theatre, to the business of playing games, applying to himself as well as to Shakespeare, also sounds uncannily apt to Gielgud, for *Prospero's Books* is no less his personal farewell to a long theatrical career as an actor.

However, it would be wrong to think of *Prospero's Books* as an altogether unselfish project for Greenaway, for his personal stakes in it are very consider-able. For one thing, throughout his career as a maker of feature films, Greenaway has taken a genuine interest in 17th-century drama, most obviously in *The Draughtsman's Contract* (1982), which owes a great deal to the Res-toration comedies of Etherege, Congreve, Wycherley, and Dryden, but also in *The Cook, The Thief, His Wife and Her Lover* (1989), which borrows freely from early Jacobean revenge drama.

In addition, the filming of *Prospero's Books* posed a technological challange to Greenaway, who has commented on the fascination of mixing conventional film production with the most advanced video post-production processes and techniques (HDTV and the computerized paintbox), and the revolution in the language of the cinema consequent upon it, issuing in

> a whole series of new ways of making pictures, which I was much more familiar with in terms of painting and draughtsmanship than I was with cinema. It was an ability primarily to reorganise the screen ratio, to play with colour in a way you can't in the cinema, and to extend and reshape the elements of the pictorial imagination. There was a time when I believed that the cinema had an ability to use all the letters of the alphabet and TV could only use the vowels. I don't believe that to be the case any more; I think TV has its own vocabulary, its own alphabet. So what I wanted to do in *Prospero's Books* is to make the first tentative steps towards an expanded cinema which uses television vocabulary but still hangs on to the cinematic idea of creating images which are bigger, noisier, louder, more engulfing than you are.[21]

It seems as if Greenaway has been inspired by Prospero-Shakespeare's potent magic to pursue every conceivable visual possibility offered by the state of the art in film and television technology in his urge to add to Shakespeare's dramatic story a 'layer' of cinematic discourse which does not count simply as cinematic adaptation in the traditional sense of the word. In Prospero's books (the books themselves no less than their cinematic realization), any ontological difference – between inner and outer, present and past, sign – whether word or image – and meaning, indeed, between what is cinematically representable and what is not – must constantly be probed and, if possible, transcended to satisfy Greenaway's ambition to recreate a cinema with the same thoroughly magical aura that it had in its childhood, when the great magician of early 20th-century cinema, George Méliès, could transform a bus into a hearse in the twinkling of an eye, when audiences would flee the auditorium in fear of trains or floods. Nothing seems finally alien to Greenaway's painterly urge to emulate by purely *visual* means the potent *verbal* magic of his ideal reflection in the mirror of *The Tempest*, Prospero-Shakespeare.

Greenaway's relationship to Shakespeare is by no means as facile and uncomplicated as that of the deferential pupil to his teacher, of the pliable son to his father, or of the weak stage producer or film director to the spirit of the playwright's words, which, in an act of hermeneutic faith, he guards over and 'translates' into theatrical or cinematic performance without loss or gain. With its inimitable, uniquely 'answerable' cinematic style, *Prospero's Books* writes *The Tempest* under erasure and stages it according to that logic of the 'dangerous supplement' which in *Of Grammatology* Derrida excavates from Rousseau's conception of writing's relation to speech, the supplement performing the double function of adding to complete and to compensate for a lack in what was supposed to have been complete in itself. Greenaway has deliberately chosen to read *The Tempest* from a third 'site' of criticism, one which is neither entirely historicist nor exclusively formalist, but which investigates the nebulous border area between Shakespeare's life and his art, between the real and the imaginary.[22] The resultant 'rewriting', *Prospero's Books*, qualifies – in terms of Harold Bloom's theory of poetic misprision – as a 'strong misreading', one which appropriates the site occupied by the original by displacing it. Grenaway is indeed a Bloomian ephebe, a late-coming 'reader' who fights an *agon* with the precursor, a struggle for life and poetic authority. One of Bloom's many renderings of the relationship of the ephebe to his precursor has it that 'the good poet steals, while the poor poet betrays an influence, borrows a voice'.[23] Greenaway betrays his own strength as a capable misreader of Shakespeare by declining to borrow his voice; on the contrary, he *returns* a Shakespearean voice and face to Prospero, an activity whose rhetorical name is *prosopopeia*.[24] By virtue of his autobiographical approach to *The Tempest*, Greenaway can insinuate into his Prospero-Shakespeare figure a personal element that shatters the traditional image of Shakespeare as impersonal artificer, defaced by himself and by accidents of literary history.

By picturing Prospero's auto-critique of the autonomous imagination and its Nietzschean will-to-power as a displaced form of Shakespearean self-representation, Greenaway liberates the potential meaning of *The Tempest* as a metafictional record of the play's own coming into being, even as, towards the end of his life and dramatic career, Shakespeare surveys the topography of his work. The non-origin of the origin, *Prospero's Books* is a palimpsestic repetition of *The Tempest*, a restaging of the original which brings out what it really meant to say but which, due to a blindness inherent in its own medium, it could only say in the displaced form of Greenaway's cinematic language.

Notes

1. See James Monaco's discussion of the ontological nature of film and its differences from other art forms, including theatre, in *How To Read a Film* (New York & Oxford: Oxford University Press, 1977), chapter I, 'Film as an Art'. The comparison of film and theatre is the exclusive subject of *Focus on Film and Theatre*, ed. James Hurt (Englewood Cliffs, New Jersey: Prentice Hall, Inc., 1974), in which I find Hurt's 'Introduction: Film/Theatre/Film/Theatre/Film', Stanley Kauffmann's 'Notes on Theatre-and-Film', and Peter Handke's 'Theatre and Film: The Misery of Comparison' particularly recommendable.

   The discussion of the relative merits of film and literature has often focused on one literary genre, that of the novel, in a comparison of its capacity for narrative with that of film. See for example Seymour Chatman, *Story and Discourse: Narrative Structure in Fiction and Film* (Ithaca: Cornell University Press, 1978), his article, 'What Novels Can Do That Films Can't (and Vice Versa)', *Critical Inquiry*, Vol. 7 (1980), and Leon Edel, 'Novel and Camera', in *The Theory of the Novel. New Essays*, ed. John Halperin (New York: Oxford University Press, 1974).

2. Adam Barker, 'A Tale of Two Magicians' (interview with Peter Greenaway), in *Sight and Sound* (September 1991), p. 28.

3. Peter Greenaway, *Prospero's Books. A Film of Shakespeare's The Tempest* (London: Chatto & Windus, 1991), p. 9.

4. Greenaway, p. 9.

5. On the possible sources of *The Tempest*, see for example Frank Kermode's introduction to the New Arden edition of *The Tempest*, ed. Frank Kermode (London: Methuen, 1954), and Kenneth Muir, *The Sources of Shakespeare's Plays* (London: Methuen, 1977), pp. 278-83.

6. For the history of the reception of *The Tempest* as well as of Shakespeare's work in general, see the introduction to *Shakespeare: The Tempest*, ed. D.J. Palmer (Casebook Series; London: MacMillan, 1968), and Arthur M. Eastman's impressive historical survey in *A Short History of Shakespearean Criticism* (New York: W.W. Norton, 1968).

7. 'Myth and Miracle', quoted from G. Wilson Knight, *The Crown of Life. Essays in Interpretation of Shakespeare's Final Plays* (London: Methuen, 1948), p. 9.

8. Knight, 'The Shakespearian Superman: A Study of *The Tempest*', in Knight, p. 204.

9. William Shakespeare, *The Tempest*, ed. by Frank Kermode (The Arden Shakespeare, London: Methuen, 1954), Epilogue, 1-20. All further references to the play are to this edition and are included in the text.

10. The concept of 'the truth of the page', which is due to the American novelist-critic Ronald Sukenick, is quoted by Brian McHale in *Postmodernist Fiction* (London and New York: Routledge, 1987), p. 198. See McHale's entire chapter 13, 'Authors: Dead and Posthumous', where he treats of that post-Modern literary dismantling of the old-style, authoritative author-God which paradoxically ends up reasserting some sort of first-principle writing instance, even if it resides in the impersonal activity of writing rather than in the authorial writing subject.

11. Cf. Greenaway's own detailed ground plan at the beginning of *Prospero's Books. A Film of Shakespeare's The Tempest* for 'Prospero's island, rebuilt in all its many parts to fit the requirements of an exiled scholar far from home, dreaming of Italy'.

12. Greenaway, p. 12.

13. 'Bien que cette nature se manifeste physiquement, elle existe entièrement dans la tête de Prospero. De même pour l'architecture. C'est pour cela que nous avons délibérément fait ces citations, ces hommages, comme la reconstitution de la bibliothèque laurentienne à Florence dessinée par Michel-Ange ou de la villa de Bomarzo avec ses monstres ou de l'église chrétienne à l'intérieur de la mosquée de Cordoue ou de la basilique Saint-Marc ... ['Even though this universe manifests itself physically, it exists entirely in the mind of Prospero. The same goes for the architecture, which is why we have deliberately made quotations and paid hommages in the way of the reconstruction of the Laurentian Library in Florens, which was designed by Michelangelo, of the Villa Bomarzo with all its monsters, of the Christian church in the interior of the mosque in Cordova, of the Basilica San Marco ...']'. Peter Greenaway in an interview with Michel Ciment, 'Une conflagration de l'art', in *Positif*, no. 368 (Octobre 1991), p. 44.

14. Kott's essay on 'Prospero's Staff', which appeared in his *Shakespeare: Our Contemporary* (1964), is quoted here from D.J. Palmer, p. 250.

15. Kott, p. 251.

16. It is significant that, derived from the Greek verb *charassein*, meaning to engrave, to stamp, to inscribe, *character* applies to letters inscribed on parchment, stone, etc., by a scribe as well as to the 'inscription' of a peculiar mental disposition on the soul of man by the supreme scribe, God.

17. Jonathan Culler, *On Deconstruction. Theory and Criticism after Structuralism* (London: Routledge & Kegan Paul, 1983), p. 92.

18. Jacques Derrida, *Of Grammatology*, transl. by Gayatri Chakravorty Spivak (Baltimore: Johns Hopkins University Press, 1976), p. 12.

19. Deriving ultimately from the Greek verb *theaomai*, meaning to look at, to contemplate, to gaze at in wonder, *theatre* designates, in the widest sense of the word, a place where something is meant to be seen. Cf. Roland Barthes' essay on 'Diderot, Brecht, Eisenstein': 'The scene, the picture, the shot, the cut-out rectangle, here we have the very *condition* that allows us to conceive theatre, painting, cinema, literature, all those arts, that is, other than music and which could be called *dioptric arts*.... The tableau (pictorial, theatrical, literary) is a pure cut-out segment with clearly defined edges, irreversible and incorruptible; everything that surrounds it is banished into nothingness, remains unnamed, while everything that it admits within its field is promoted into essence, into light, into view'. Roland Barthes, *Image — Music — Text* (London: Fontana, 1977), p. 70.

20. Cf. Jacques Derrida's reading of Antonin Artaud's attempt on the entire concept and history of Western theatre, the theatre of representation, 'The Theatre of Cruelty and the Closure of Representation', in Jacques Derrida, *Writing and Difference* (London: Routledge & Kegan Paul, 1978), pp. 232-50.

21. Adam Barker, p. 28.

22. Incidentally, the same approach is adopted by Steven Soderbergh in his film, *Kafka* (1992), in which one is never quite sure whether one witnesses an episode in the life of the historical Franz Kafka or in that of the fictional protagonist of *The Trial*, Joseph K.

23. Harold Bloom, *The Anxiety of Influence. A Theory of Poetry* (London: Oxford University Press, 1973), p. 31.

24. Prosopopeia (personification) is one of the time-honoured tropes of clasical rhetoric. It signifies the metaphorical activity by which an inanimate object, a deceased person, or an abstract concept is endowed with life or human attributes and feelings. In an essay on 'Autobiography as De-Facement' (1979), Paul de Man argues that prosopopeia is 'the fiction of an apostrophe to an absent, deceased, or voiceless entity, which posits the possibility of the latter's reply and confers upon it the power of speech. Voice assumes mouth, eye, and finally face, a chain that is manifest in the etymology of the trope's name, *prosopon poiein*, to confer a mask or a face (*prosopon*). Prosopopeia is the trope of autobiography'. Paul de Man, *The Rhetoric of Romanticism* (New York: Columbia University Press, 1984), pp. 75-76.

The Contributors

Susanne Fabricius is External Lecturer in the Department of Film, TV and Communication, the University of Copenhagen, Denmark.

Ib Johansen is Associate Professor of English, the University of Aarhus, Denmark.

Bernice W. Kliman is Professor of English, Nassau Community College, SUNY, New York, USA.

Michael Mullin is Associate Professor, University of Illinois at Urbana-Champaign, USA.

Per Serritslev Petersen is Associate Professor of English, the University of Aarhus, Denmark.

Claus Schatz-Jacobsen is External Lecturer in the Department of English, the University of Odense, Denmark.

William E. Sheidley is Professor of English at the University of Connecticut (on leave), and Assistant Professor of English at the United States Air Force Academy, USA.

Steven Shelburne is Associate Professor of English, Centenary College of Louisiana, Shreveport, LA., USA.

Michael Skovmand is Associate Professor of English, University of Aarhus, Denmark.